Local Color

Gwen Keane

Deltaville, Virginia 23043

Copyright © 2015 by Gwen Keane

All rights reserved. No part of this publication may be reproduced, distributed or transmitted in any form or by any means, including photocopying, recording, or other electronic or mechanical methods, without the prior written permission of the publisher, except in the case of brief quotations embodied in critical reviews and certain other noncommercial uses permitted by copyright law. For permission requests, write to the publisher, addressed "attention: permissions coordinator," at the address below.

High Tide Publications, Inc.
1000 Bland Point
Deltaville, Virginia 23043

www.hightidepublications.com
Quantity sales. Special discounts are available on quantity purchases by
corporations, associations, and others. For details, contact the "Special Sales Department" at the address above.

Local Color/Gwen Keane, 1st ed.

Printed in the United States of America
Local Color:

ISBN 978-0692503690

Dedicated to Bobbi Gaskins Weeks

My lifetime friend who helped create all of these wonderful memories.
Thanks for always being there, girlfriend.

Table of Contents

Section I: Barefoot And Free

1 That Was Just The Way It Was	3
2 Grandma And Granddaddy	8
3 Ditchley House Ghosts	18
4 Places Little Girls Dare Not Go!	25
5 A Lesson In Generosity	33
6 Sundays	39
7 Outdoor Play	45
8 Growing Up In The Seafood Business	54
9 Captain Pruett	60
10 The Curry Family	64
11 Elementary School Days	67
12 The Child Sailors	74
13 The Fish Hunt	81

Section II: From Bare Feet To Ball Gowns

95

14 Beauty Queens	
15 Saturday Night In Kilmarnock	102
16 Annual Community Events	107
17 The Dress	112
18 Ballroom Dancing	117
19 Lifetime Friends A Local Custom	123
20 Time For A Perm	126

Section III: Places And People Make The Community

21	Mama No And Daddy Wil	133
22	Cousin Pearl	139
23	The Eubank Family	148
24	The Adams Brides	152
25	Miss Enid And Family	158
26	Lou Baker	164
27	Claudine Curry Smith	168
28	Born Into The Funeral Business	172
29	Ditchley Landscape	178
30	Some More Equal Than Others	183

About The Author — 190

Index Of Photographs — 193

INTRODUCTION

Knock, knock!

Who's there?

During the 1950's the Northern Neck boys played softball and the girls dreamed of being crowned queens, just like that night in 1895 when Mr. John Palmer crowned Miss Cora Brent the first queen of the local Holly Ball.

The Menhaden industry was in its prime.

People, like the Eubank Family and their generosity, helped form the community, in ways I didn't understand; sometimes funny, sometimes tragic.

These experiences and people shaped the life I lived, four miles from Kilmarnock.

Section I:
BAREFOOT AND FREE

Ditchley, my personal "rabbit hole" made me feel like Alice in Wonderland, but I never wished to escape. Intuitively I knew this special place is where special people lived. Life could not have been better.

1	That Was Just the Way It Was
2	Grandma and Granddaddy
3	Ditchley House Ghosts
4	Places Little Girls Dare Not Go
5	A Lesson in Generosity
6	Sundays
7	Outdoor Play
8	Growing Up in the Seafood Business
9	Captain Pruett
10	The Curry Family
11	Elementary School Days
12	The Child Sailor
13	The Fish Hunt

1

THAT WAS JUST THE WAY IT WAS

Photo 1 – The Road to Ditchley

My childhood occurred during the years of segregation, when black people were forced to use separate waiting rooms in doctors' offices, were not allowed to attend the one movie theater in Kilmarnock, couldn't be served food at the local restaurant in town, and were not allowed to order food or sit at the soda fountain counters of the two drug stores. That was just the way life was back then.

My childhood community, Ditchley, is surrounded by a shoreline of white sand. It hugs the edge of the Chesapeake Bay, in Northumberland County, Virginia.

As a child, I lay in a tester bed overlooking Prentise Creek, and watched the flecks of early morning sunlight sparkle above the water like fairy dust. My bed, once owned by the Lee family of Virginia, has travelled with me throughout my life.

On Route 200, four miles outside of the Kilmarnock corporate limits, is Ditchley road. The road passes through a residential area, and open space before the *glades* appear, a forest of tall pine trees that once served as a physical barrier to divide the white residents, who lived on waterfront property, and the black residents, who lived inland.

In the 1950's, the black residents of Ditchley, mostly watermen, independently crabbed and fished, worked on commercial fishing boats, crewed on the boats owned by Crittenden Gaskins, or my grandfather Carter Keane. My grandfather owned Ditchley Packing Company, a seafood plant.

The inland homes were constructed of brick or white clapboard and, surprisingly the few that weren't painted over the years, have still survived. A recent ride through my old community confirmed much hasn't changed. The juke joint at the top of the hill on the corner of Route 200 and Ditchley road no longer exists. It had the reputation for inspiring Saturday night brawls. On the way to church on Sunday mornings, my grandfather would drive carefully, being fully aware we might need to stop and move a body from the road, a leftover from the night before.

Today there are only residents in Ditchley. Guarded by weeds that continue to grow on both sides of the hard surfaced road, the inland community retains the look of rural countryside that has escaped change, except for the addition of a large gated estate and a caretaker's home. Past the turn off that goes to Cobbs Hall, drivers approach a recognizable curve, and a high bank that shields a former school house built for the black community. Today it remains a private residence.

A few of the inland houses are deserted, but most are still standing. A house trailer has been added, something we never saw when I was a child. As I drive past the former Curry family home, I begin to wonder what the original owners, Minnie and Lonnie, might say if they were to see their old front door painted blood red. The land across from their house is still vacant. It was the only place kids in the black community had to play ball.

I recall the day daddy and I saw children playing in the middle of Ditchley Road. They all began to scatter when they heard the sound of our car. I asked daddy how black mothers knew which child belonged to which mother. Showing irritation at me for having asked the question, he said, "Well, I guess it is no different than white mothers knowing their children."

I never questioned why a part of our society existed for whites only. As naïve as it seems, I saw the larger community as a place where everyone was expected to use good manners and respect all adults, regardless of their skin color or financial status. Many years would pass before I questioned the value system I had been taught versus what I remembered being practiced.

Our world in Ditchley and the Northern Neck was small. In our home, we had a Zenith black-and-white television set my grandfather purchased from Mr. Payne's store on Main Street in Kilmarnock. We could watch a show on one of three networks. Two were broadcast from Richmond and one from

Norfolk. The networks stopped broadcasting at 11 p.m., but that was not a concern because watermen, farmers, and their families went to bed early.

We didn't travel far or often. We stayed close to home in the Northern Neck. If we wanted to go to Middlesex County or Newport News we got on the White Stone ferry. We visited Richmond two or three times a year. The Downing Bridge, between Warsaw and Tappahannock, opened in 1927 and brought people from Richmond who chose to make the Northern Neck their second home.

An older adult friend of mine described her life in Kilmarnock before the Downing Bridge was built. She said locals felt the Richmond people thought of us as being ignorant country folks who had never seen city lights. On the opening day of the bridge she recalled how anxious people were in Kilmarnock, anticipating the pending infiltration of city folks. Local gossip suggested the supposed infiltrators thought people in the Northern Neck were naked savages.

Welcome to Local Color – stories about a rural community with a special attraction, where everyone knew everyone and could recite each family's ancestry. We lived in a small piece of a a place where we had sent loved ones to war, and thought those who survived would surely come back home to the Northern Neck.

Photo 2   My paternal grandparents with my father (in diapers)

2.

GRANDMA AND GRANDDADDY

When I was four, my parents divorced, and my paternal grandparents raised me. I know this might seem hard to understand, but I don't remember the word race spoken at home. I do recall Grandma saying something like, "If God didn't want us to live separately, he would not have created different races." That was her reasoning, and she wasn't alone. Yet she always showed compassion and kindness towards all people.

On cold winter days, I recall Grandma telephoning Granddaddy at his seafood plant and offering the men workers hot soup. Granddaddy sent the men to the house, and while seated at the kitchen table with the black men, I watched Grandma fill their soup bowls. Her generosity was not limited just to the men who worked for us.

One day a black woman, Mattie, who lived inland came to our house asking for Grandma. She wanted to start a little community store, and she needed financial help. My grandmother, who never had extra money, somehow came up with $30 for Mattie. From the day that community store opened its doors, whenever we needed a loaf of bread or anything else the store might have, Grandma would say "Let's run up to Mattie's."

Grandma, a nurturer and homemaker, not only raised my father and me, she and Granddaddy also raised two of her nephews.

Although we didn't have a lot of money, we never discussed the topic. Grandma knew how to stretch a dollar. Sometimes her conservative methods embarrassed me, like the day she went to the county dump and came home with a pair of well-worn black shoes. I watched as she dipped a brush into a little can of red paint, and on Sunday morning she wore the brush-streaked shoes to church. Oftentimes her stockings had runs in them, but she would make sure the runs were put on the inside of her legs, and she assured me no one would notice. Grandma never spent money unnecessarily except when I wanted something.

When I reached the age of twelve I wanted new bedroom furniture, curtains, rugs, and a bedspread. I also wanted a television set in my room and a Princess-style telephone. I never got the television or the phone, but I got the bedroom set.

On Main Street in Kilmarnock Monday through Saturday a large panel truck would park in front of the old Safeway store. The truck owner was Mr. Junior Harvey, whose mother was Grandma's best friend and whose father was the mayor of Kilmarnock. Mr. Harvey sold furniture. One day after grocery shopping with Grandma, I returned to the car while she spoke to Mr. Harvey. She motioned for me to join her and then said I should go inside the truck and select a bedroom suite. At home that night, Grandma and I flipped through the pages of the Sears and Roebuck catalog and chose new accessories for my bedroom.

Years later I would learn how Grandma had paid for the furniture and the accessories. She sold the clothes I had outgrown that my other grandmother had bought for me. She also sold some furniture we didn't need. Each month she would go to Kilmarnock, find Mr. Harvey, and give him a cash payment towards the furniture. I have no idea how many years it took to pay off this debt, but she managed to do it.

My grandmother, a woman who stood five feet four inches tall, had thick strawberry blonde hair she wore in a bun. When angry, Grandma would blink her piercing blue eyes. I most remember her great sense of humor and how much she enjoyed playing jokes on me, like the night she went upstairs and hid in the bathroom wearing a skeleton mask. I entered, and she jumped out. When I screamed, she laughed, and we hugged. It was close to Halloween, and in my community adults as well as kids dressed up. Grandma had never intended to scare me.

Whenever threatened by a thunderstorm, Grandma disappeared into the basement. I always knew where to find her, sitting on the basement steps in total darkness. She insisted the television set be unplugged, and if the phone rang it went unanswered. Although she loved animals, not even the dog could be petted during a storm. According to Grandma, dogs drew lightning. Even today whenever I hear thunder, I get nervous; but I still pet my dogs.

Grandma never cared about clothes. Most of her clothes she made by hand without a pattern. She would take a dress or a skirt and put it on top of a piece of material, then cut around it. Once satisfied with the shape, she threaded her needle and sewed it. She rarely bought clothes. There were a few exceptions-- a new dress to wear to the annual banker's Christmas party held at the Tides Inn, a dress she wore to my wedding, and a navy blue suit that she kept for serious events, like the Parent Teachers Association (PTA) meeting. The rest of her wardrobe was hand-made, unless someone gave her a gift.

Granddaddy always dressed like a gentleman. He only wore name-brand clothes. Even his everyday winter shirts were made by Pendleton. His long-sleeved dress shirts required cuff links. My grandfather did not like change. A Buick, the only brand of car he ever owned, was purchased locally from T. D. McGinnes in Kilmarnock. I felt special accompanying him to Kilmarnock to select the new family car from a choice of two.

My grandfather once accepted a project manager's job that required him to work in Norfolk, Virginia during the week. On Sunday afternoons that winter, he would take his big brown leather suitcase from the closet and carefully pack his white shirts, bow ties, and two suits. Everything he wore, including a brown felt fedora hat, had to meet his personal standard.

After Granddaddy left on Sunday afternoon, Grandma would begin to lock up the house. We never had house keys. To lock the front door, we used the dead bolt and a sliding bolt on both the kitchen and back doors. Before darkness the entire house would be locked up, and then Grandma insisted we go to bed.

Grandma, a very punctual person, once delayed feeding the stray cats. After dark when she put down a pan of table scraps at the back door, she heard a loud stomping sound in back of her. She ran inside and directed me to go upstairs. Then she called our neighbor Mr. Gaskins, and told him a man wearing boots had run across the back yard. In the bedroom I waited for Grandma. After she came, I helped her slide the dresser in front of the door. When we heard Mr. Gaskins arrive, Grandma raised the bedroom window and called down to him. He yelled back he thought the noise had come from a big buck he had seen standing in our field.

Mr. Gaskins failed to convince Grandma that the noise she heard had been caused by a deer. So, from that night forward, we slept with the dresser against the bedroom door. It was a long winter, and both of us were glad when Granddaddy's job was over.

Grandma lived to be ninety-nine. She never wanted to be a burden to anyone, and she always tried to be cheerful, regardless of the circumstances. Even if Grandma didn't understand what caused my mother or me to be unhappy, she always managed to make us feel good. Mama used to say, "If I am upset or depressed, all I have to do is call Mom, because she always knows how to make me feel better."

When Granddaddy was alive, he too benefitted from Grandma's positive attitude. At the supper table she listened, and if she thought he was upset or his day hadn't gone well, she filtered the conversation and thus delayed delivering the bad news. That was part of her duty as a wife, to make life pleasant for the family.

꧁꧂

After Grandma broke her hip at age ninety, she went to live at the Lancashire Nursing Home in Kilmarnock. Each evening I telephoned her, and we chatted.

She had been at the Lancashire for just a few days when she told me, "My feet get cold, and it really is hard to climb over the bed railings, walk to the dresser, and get my socks. But the worst part is the return trip, because it takes so much strength to climb back into bed."

After I hung up the phone that night I cried and told my husband Grandma had lost her mind. We visited her that next weekend and witnessed her walking down the hall aided by a walker.

"Grandma, you're walking." I shouted.

She picked up the walker and held it over her head.

"Of course I'm walking. I just use this damn thing to keep these people quiet."

I discovered Grandma had been climbing over the bed railing to get her socks. She had gotten caught. The nurses complained to her doctor. Dr. Gravatt said "I've known Emily Keane for more than fifty years, and if she wants to do something, she is going to do it. So, just leave her alone."

During her later years, Grandma's short-term memory began to fail. Sometimes she would ask for Lettie, the black woman who helped raise her and her seven siblings at the plantation Bushfield in Westmoreland County. Grandma often spoke of Lettie being present in her room.

A week before Grandma died I visited her on a Saturday. The nursing staff had called me at home in DC and said Grandma refused to eat.

I entered her room and found her lying on her back staring at the ceiling. Her cheerfulness was gone. I kissed her and asked if she would go to the hospital, because she was dehydrated. She shook her head NO. I then told her I loved her so much, but I didn't want her to be uncomfortable. She remained silent. Her skin color was pale except for brown spots and bruises. The arthritis in her hands had made her fingers curl. She looked so frail and tense. I felt she wanted to say good-bye but wouldn't because she knew I would cry. I had to give reassurance I could accept her wishes. I knew it was time for me to say what needed to be said. I took a deep breath and found the strength to ask, "Are you ready to die?" And she nodded YES. I kissed her, stroked her forehead, and said, "I will always love you, and I will be fine." I left her room, never to look back, and drove to DC, crying the entire three-hour trip.

I told my husband, "Grandma has decided to die." He didn't believe me. At the end of the week, while away on government travel, my husband called and said he had gotten a telephone call from Grandma's caregiver Matilda. She reported Grandma was much improved and had eaten a nice supper. Two hours later I got the call she had died. That was Grandma. She had made up her mind it was time to die, and she did it her way.

Grandma and Granddaddy met at Bushfield when he helped his uncle, a waterman. Granddaddy was a city boy who grew up in Bladensburg, Maryland and studied architecture at George Washington University. After he and Grandma were married, he returned home to his maternal roots in the Northern Neck as the Manager of the East Coast Utilities Company. He brought the first electric lights to the Neck. Over the years, he did many other things to earn a living. His seafood plant provided the fresh fish, oysters, and crabs for his cousin's restaurant, The Flagship, in Washington, D.C. His engineering expertise helped him obtain a project manager position with the Campbell Soup Company to install the first oyster-shucking machine in Norfolk, Virginia. He worked as a land appraiser for the Veterans Administration. He installed both in-ground commercial and residential swimming pools. He also performed draftsman services for home owners and businesses. A board member of the Bank of Lancaster for thirty years, he served as the Vice-President for ten.

At supper one evening, Granddaddy announced he was going to run for the Northumberland County Board of Supervisors. He won that election and served eight years. Shortly after winning his first election, he toured the black elementary school on Route 200. We had a very somber supper that night. Granddaddy, who shook his head in disgust, described the deplorable conditions of the school. He vowed to give the black community a new school. And he did, with support from the other supervisors.

Although Granddaddy was very much a public figure, he had a quiet demeanor. But when he spoke, I listened. People used to say my grandfather adored me. My grandfather made me feel special, so I accompanied him whenever given the chance. He and I would take his old dead-rise boat out to check on the oyster shore. I prided myself on being Granddaddy's little helper, whether it meant retrieving something from the cabin of the boat, or holding the end of a tape measure while he surveyed land.

In the summer I always looked forward to our evening ride to the Kilmarnock Drug Store to buy a half-gallon of vanilla ice cream. Granddaddy would reach into his back pocket and take out his worn billfold and hand me $1.00. He carried a little plastic change purse in his front pants pocket. That is where he got the four cents needed for tax. Back at home I complained to Grandma about having to always buy vanilla ice cream when I preferred peach. But I knew better than to complain to Granddaddy.

In the summer of 1966, my grandfather wasn't feeling well. He and Grandma took me to Richmond and got me settled in at the Wilson Inn, a facility run by the Methodist Church for young working girls and girls attending business school. I was enrolled in Commonwealth Business College for a nine-month course in stenography. Two weeks after I started school, Granddaddy was diagnosed with colon cancer. I visited him each afternoon after class at the hospital in Richmond. In June I graduated and came home for the summer. I was engaged and planned to marry in September. Granddaddy was supposed to give me away; he never got the opportunity. He died August 24.

When I visited him earlier in the day, I knew the situation had worsened. Being young and scared, I just couldn't allow myself to sit and wait. I drove home and at four a.m. the doctor called.

He said, "Mr. Keane has succumbed."

"Is he dead?" I asked.

Richard, a nephew my grandparents had raised, said he was with Granddaddy on the eve of his death and had listened to him call my name.

My first experience with grief happened when my grandfather died. Suddenly I knew the real meaning of the word forever. For years I kept the memories of all the sadness I had felt during the last year of Granddaddy's life tucked away. I wanted to remember only the good times and all of the life skills he taught me.

After Granddaddy died, we found three wills he had signed during his year of illness. The first will set aside money to be used for my education. The second will decreased the amount of money because a semester had ended. The third will, signed after I had graduated, left everything to Grandma. My grandfather's conscious efforts to ensure that my education would be paid for reaffirmed what I already knew, that he loved me very much.

3

DITCHLEY HOUSE GHOSTS

Photo 3   Ditchley House

The Ditchley house, built in 1765 for Richard Lee's great-grandson Kendall Lee, included approximately 300 acres that were delineated by Prentice and Dividing Creeks. In 1840, the house was expanded with the addition of a wing and in 1935 with a matching wing, and a kitchen. Ditchley House remained in the Richard Lee family until 1789, when James Ball, Jr., the husband of Kendall Lee's aunt, Lettice Lee, bought it. Around 1920 my great-great-grandmother, Cora Lee Carter Keane, a descendent of the Virginia Lee family and the mother of my grandfather Carter Martin Keane, bought Ditchley House.

My paternal grandparents, Carter Keane and his wife Emily Detrick Keane, moved from Philadelphia and into *Ditchley House* to care for his ailing mother, Cora Keane. In 1932, after my great grandmother died, my grandfather and his siblings inherited the house and surrounding property.

The estate was listed for $25,000. Jessie Ball duPont, the third wife of Alfred I. duPont[1] (who was raised in Balls Neck on Dividing Creek), purchased it for $18,000 from the Keane family.

After the property sold in 1935, my grandfather oversaw the *Ditchley House* restoration project. This began a long-term business relationship between Grandaddy and Jessie Ball duPont. Until his death in 1967, my grandfather took care of local duPont business matters, including *Ditchley House* and the community water system provided to all residents free of charge by Mrs. duPont. These also included inquiries from local citizens asking my grandfather to request money on their behalf, whether it was for a church or for someone's child needing money for college. It was common for people to show up and ask to speak to my grandfather. He always listened, and if he felt the request was valid, he sent it on to Mrs. DuPont.

Bobbi Gaskins and I grew up together in Ditchley. We rarely wore shoes in the summer while playing on oyster shell piles or walked on oyster shell lanes in our bare feet. Cuts and bruises were discussed and shared daily, as if we were doing show-and- tell time at school. We believed ourselves to be adventuresome while roaming freely throughout the

---

[1] Alfred Irénée du Pont was an American industrialist, financier, philanthropist and a member of the influential Du Pont family. Mrs. DuPont married him in 1921.

community. We were unaware that Bobbi's mother and my grandma always kept a close eye on us. A single yell of "Bobbi," or a whistle for me got our immediate attention.

One year we both received ball-bearing roller skates (the kind that fit over your shoes and required a key to adjust them) from Santa Claus. After the discovery of a large paved area in front of the caretaker's home at *Ditchley House,* roller-skating became a favorite pastime for us. We would skate on Ditchley Road, and while wearing skates, jump a ditch and continue on the narrow brick path that merged into the long brick driveway.

Although we were adventuresome, we were not brave little girls. Maybe that is why the memory of seeing the ghost is as vivid today as it was more than fifty years ago. One day after a fun afternoon of skating, we realized the time had come to head home. We stopped to tighten our skates in front of *Ditchley House*. We both happened to look up at a window where a woman with long black hair and an expressionless face stood holding a vase.

I asked, "What is that?"

Bobbi said, "Run."

Scared out of our wits, we fell several times before we arrived at my house. Our legs were covered in blood, and our knees were skinned as we ran into the house yelling for Grandma.

She had heard our voices and the noise caused by our skates as we tried to walk across the hardwood floors. Through lots of sobs, we told our story.

Grandma tried to console us by saying she had seen the ghost many times, and that it wouldn't harm us.

A ghost! We were horrified, yet I had been brought up on Grandma's stories about the ghosts at *Bushfield*, her family's plantation, and her remembrances of living at *Ditchley House* with ghosts. She always got very serious when telling the stories.

⁂

Convinced ghosts lived at *Ditchley House*, Grandma said the experiences had been so frequent no one paid any attention to them. In the upstairs *Blue Room*, bed covers were pulled off during the night. Visiting family members would insist on staying in another bedroom. In the middle of the night, a clanking sound would be heard, as if chains were being dragged on the steps of the stairway. However, when anyone tried to find the cause of the noise, it stopped.

Late one night, after my grandparents and family members returned home from the annual Holly Ball, they sat in the parlor waiting for the return of a daughter, Esther Lee, who had attended the ball with a date. When they heard the front door open, slam shut, and footsteps running up the stairs, Granddaddy walked into the hallway and yelled for Esther Lee. There was no answer. He went upstairs to the *Blue Room,* and after a thorough search, when no one was found he returned to the parlor. Early morning, when Esther Lee returned home, she was asked if she had returned home earlier in the evening. "NO," she replied.

Because of the ancestral relationship to the Lee family, I felt connected to *Ditchley House* and to Mrs. duPont, to whom we often referred as *Cousin Jessie*. I used to accompany my grandparents on the long trips to *Nemours*, the famous duPont estate in Wilmington, Delaware where Granddaddy would meet with Mrs. duPont and establish a schedule for her future visits to *Ditchley House.*

The year before Bobbi and I encountered the ghost, I had been sitting in a car with Granddaddy in front of *Ditchley House* awaiting the arrival of Mrs. duPont. I watched her large black limo slowly move up the winding driveway and park in front of the old Georgian plantation house. Mrs. duPont, dressed in a full-length brown mink coat, exited the limo. At first I only noticed her coat, but my attention quickly diverted to the chauffeur, who had started to remove hatboxes and luggage from the trunk. Granddaddy said Mrs. duPont's visit would be short, but to me a short visit meant a change of clean underwear and a playsuit stuffed into a paper grocery bag.

Invited to sit in the parlor, I waited while Granddaddy and Mrs. duPont met. In the room amongst the many antiques, tapestries, and large oil paintings, I noticed a beautiful red glass object shaped like a fish on the mantle.

The object, out of my reach, forced me to comply with the "no touch rule I had been taught.

More than fifty years passed before Bobbi, who lived in North Carolina, and I, who lived in Washington, D.C., attended the bi-annual Dividing Creek Association community picnic and toured Ditchley House. On the waterfront side of the estate, we joined the people who mingled and talked in front of the tables covered with dishes of food. Yet I could only remember a few of the people in attendance from my childhood. The other smiling faces belonged to strangers. Finally the tour line formed. While standing in line, a conversation ignited between Bobbi and me about the day we had seen the ghost. Behind us stood the wife of the caretaker, who began sharing her own ghost story, as she recalled the day she and her little girl had gone into Ditchley House and had seen the ghost of a woman appear at the foot of the stairs. The line began to move, and therefore I chose not to ask the woman any questions about her experience.

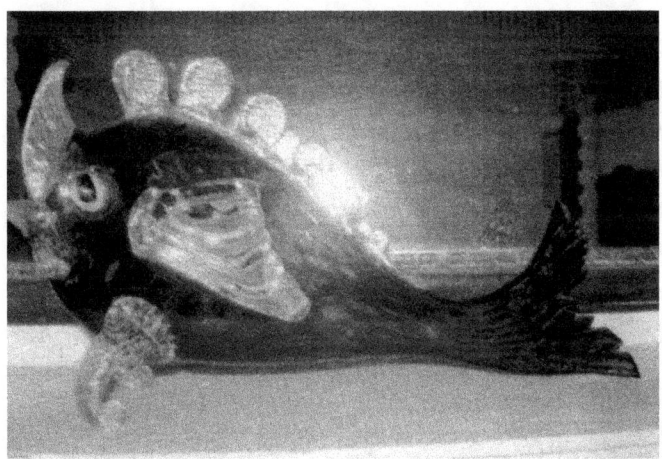

Photo 4   Red Fish that is the subject of this chapter

At the start of the tour, I felt like someone on a mission. I wanted to know if I would still see the red fish as being a beautiful object. Once we entered the parlor, I expected to find the fish on the mantle, but after my eyes carefully examined all contents in the room, I accepted the obvious--the red fish was gone. Later during the tour, I found the red fish on the mantle upstairs in the *Blue Room*. Yes, the Murano glass object remained beautiful, but I wondered who had moved it?

Several months later when I met the caretaker of *Ditchley House,* I asked him if he had ever seen any ghosts. He said "no" but did recall an incident when some electricians working in the kitchen saw a little boy dressed in colonial clothes standing in the doorway. They had quickly packed up their tools and left.

I shared my red fish story with him, and he informed me the fish had recently fallen off the mantle and had broken, but he had saved the pieces. He thought the vibration from an airplane must have caused the fish to fall. Of course, he may have been right, yet maybe Grandma had been right to believe ghosts live on at *Ditchley House*.

Mrs. duPont died in 1970. Her will created the Ditchley Trust to maintain the house and its 161 acres for lifetime use by the specified family members she named. Maintaining the house became a financial nightmare. In 2010, the trustees declared the house, with a deteriorating heating system, as being uninhabitable. A court order mandated the house, acreage, and furnishings all be transferred to the Alfred I. duPont Foundation by March 22, 2013.

4

PLACES LITTLE GIRLS DARE NOT GO!

Photo 5 My father. I am wearing the red cowboy boots, gun and holster he gave me for my fifth birthday.

Mama said, "Yes," and up the road I went with daddy. What a special day! I had dressed for the occasion, wearing my Roy Rogers cowgirl dress, a Davey Crockett raccoon hat, and the red cowboy boots daddy had given me on my fifth birthday.

Eager to leave, I climbed into the front seat of daddy's 1950 blue Buick, settling in with the stale cigarette smoke and other lifeless odors. Loud noises from under the hood of the car emerged. Daddy revved up the engine, an indicator of his impatience. I had been slow to close the car door.

"Now honey, our first stop is the Log Cabin, and I want you to promise your old daddy that you will not go home and tell your mama where I took you today."

"No daddy. I won't tell."

Daddy, who always liked to drive fast, approached each curve with one foot pressed hard on the gas pedal. His right hand clutched the steering wheel as he rested his left elbow on the windowsill and puffed his cigarette.

Seated next to him on the passenger side, I began sliding back and forth in motion with the car's movement as we bounced in and out of the deep holes in the dirt parking lot. Having so much fun, I felt as if I were on a carnival ride.

Daddy parked in front of a building made of white and brown logs. I then knew we must be at the Log Cabin. Even though Grandma wasn't with us, I still heard her say, "No one of good raising goes to that Log Cabin. It's nothing but a "joint." Daddy, who did have "good raising," never listened to Grandma or anyone else. Being his own person, what others thought or expected of Daddy didn't bother him at all.

A pool table had been placed inside the Log Cabin on the far right side of the room under the shadow of a green metal light. Daddy led me over to the opposite side of the room where a bar extended across the entire wall. In front of the bar there had been chrome barstools covered in red vinyl. You could spin the red seat with a single touch. But my fun got interrupted by Daddy.

"Come on girl, get up here."

Now I could see Mr. Winstead, the "joint" owner, who stood behind the bar.

"Whatcha gonna have, Paul?"

"Oh, give me a beer and go easy on the head."

"And how about your little girl here? Whatcha wanna get for her?"

"Ah hell, give her a cup of coffee, but make sure it has lots of sugar and cream."

Mr. Winstead smiled, then turned around to face the wall and began to fill the order.

Bored, I twirled around on the stool and, using the toes of my new red boots, kicked the front of the bar.

I listened to Mr. Winstead talk -- something about bad weather and how it hurt fishing. How could bad weather hurt fishing? I fished in the rain with my grandparents on Sunday, and we caught a lot of spot and flounder.

When daddy finished his beer, he got down off the stool.

"Come on girl. We've got places to go and people to see."

Once outside of town, daddy began to speed, turning off the main road and driving down a long dirt lane. He stopped in front of a house that looked as if no one lived there, although there were chickens in the yard. Daddy had said we were going to visit Aunt Janie. I wondered who this "Aunt Janie" was, because neither Grandma nor Mama had ever mentioned her.

With no hesitation daddy opened his car door and said I should come with him. I hesitated, though, when I saw a big rooster on the other side of the car window, but then I decided to just follow daddy, who bravely walked right past all those chickens and the rooster.

As we approached the front door, I noticed it opening slowly, and I saw the face of a very old black woman peeping out. I continued to follow daddy as he walked towards her.

She yelled. "Come in here, Paul. Come in and bring that young 'un with you."

Once inside the house, I could see the old woman bent over and leaning against a stick. She wore a rag wrapped around her head and smoked something that looked like a corncob rather than a pipe.

"Aunt Janie, this is little Gwen."

"Lordy, Lordy, Paul. Ain't she a pretty thing? Just look at those big brown eyes. Come here, child. Come let Aunt Janie give you a good look."

I slowly left my daddy's side and walked toward the old black woman, who was dressed in layers of tattered clothing. Once I got close, I noticed her shoes were men's work boots minus shoelaces. Aunt Janie now looked down at me and squeezed my shoulder with her fingers.

"My sight ain't too good, young 'un. I knows you is pretty, because your mama is a pretty thing. God knows you don't take after this hard-headed rascal."

With money in his hand, daddy walked towards us. Aunt Janie released her hand from my shoulder and grabbed the paper money. With closed fingers, she formed a tight fist.

"Come on, young 'un. I got somethin' here to show you."

I followed the old woman into her bedroom and stood at the foot of her bed while she lifted the mattress corner and stuffed the money in a hole.

"Young 'un, this here is my secret place where nobody can get my money. It's safe here 'cause I can watch it and sleep on it."

Daddy, whom we had left in the hallway, hollered for us.

"What are you two doing back there? Come on, Aunt Janie. I don't have all day."

Aunt Janie, who stopped stroking the fur on my raccoon hat, spoke softly.

"We need to go now, and don't you let Aunt Janie down and go tell anybody about my hiding spot.

Daddy and I followed Aunt Janie through a dark entrance that led to the cellar. On the last step I jumped off onto a dirt floor and followed her to a table in the middle of the room. Using the table to steady herself, Aunt Janie leaned forward, and I watched her light an oil lamp, making her wrinkled face glow. Then, like in a scary movie, in a deep voice she demanded, "Sit down, sit down." Once seated, daddy and I waited for Aunt Janie to bring the three glasses she had removed from a corner cupboard. On her second trip she brought two jugs to the table.

"Oh young 'un, I have got somethin' here good for you. This here is my homemade peach brandy. It's soooo good, it makes you want to crow like that damn old rooster out yonder."

Her long, bony fingers picked up a jug, and she poured the brandy into a glass.

After handing it to me, I lifted the glass and sniffed.

"Peaches, I love peaches." Then I tasted the brandy.

"What you think, young 'un? You like old Aunt Janie's drink?"

"Yes ma'am," I nodded.

Aunt Janie chuckled, poured a drink from the other jug, and gave it to daddy.

Then she poured herself a glass of peach brandy. Daddy, who wasted no time emptying his glass, decided the moment had come for us to leave. With Aunt Janie in the lead, we climbed the cellar stairs and walked out of the old woman's house.

We got back in the car, and daddy turned on the engine.

"Hold on baby, you gonna see some chickens fly."

Daddy shoved the gear into reverse, backed up hurriedly, and then shifted into first. Off we sped, paying no attention to the frightened chickens fluttering away from the speeding car. I turned around and looked back. Aunt Janie stood in the doorway, stomped her feet, laughed as she threw her head back, and paused before waving good-bye to the rising dust.

At the end of the lane daddy turned onto Route 200. Three miles down the road we stopped at Walter Harris'

House, where Mr. Walter, as I had been taught to call my elders, stood in the yard next to Sadie, his old work horse.

"Hey, Paul. What you been up to?"

Daddy started to answer, when Mr. Walter's wife, Miss Fidelia, appeared at the back door.

"You all come on in."

Daddy said, "Come on, baby. Fidelia hasn't seen you in a long time." Mr. Walter told us to go on ahead while he put Sadie away.

Miss Fidelia, who had been cooking, stood in the open doorway and lifted the corner of her apron, to wipe the flour from her forehead. We were then led into the living room.

"My goodness Paul, this here young 'un has grown. And look at those fancy red cowboy boots and that raccoon hat. Ain't them somethin' else? Now Paul, you shouldn't keep this young 'un away so long. How you been, Paul?

"Oh Fidelia, I've been fine, but right now I sure could use a cold beer and some of your piano playing."

"Okay. Just give me a minute."

Miss Fidelia disappeared into the kitchen, and returned with a beer for daddy and a hot chocolate for me. A piano sat in front of the picture window on the other side of the room. Miss Fidelia, a very large woman, made the floor vibrate as she walked across the room.

Seated on the piano bench, her butt hung over both ends. But once she started to pound that keyboard, I forgot about the threat of this jolly woman being swallowed up by a weakened floor. Those were the happiest sounds I had ever heard.

Then Mr. Walter came in and joined us on the sofa. We tried to keep pace with Miss Fidelia's music, our legs flopping up and down while our toes tapped against the hardwood floor.

When the music stopped, daddy dutifully announced it was time to go

On the way home, daddy didn't drive fast nor did we talk much. After the car stopped, I jumped out and ran towards the house yelling "Mama, Mama, you'll never guess where daddy took me today."

5

A Lesson in Generosity

Photo 6 Abandoned house on Route 200 that is the subject of A Lesson in Generosity

My parents divorced when I was four years old. I was a very loved and spoiled only child who escaped the scars often caused by a divorce. Love conquered my insecurities, and thus I learned life values--especially those found in a rural community like the Northern Neck, where people matter.

My Grandparents, Grandma Sue and Grandpa Ted, owned a printing business on F and 9th Streets in Washington, D.C. Grandpa Ted ran the printing press while Grandma Sue, the CEO, solicited classified printing jobs from the Department of Defense.

My visits to Washington, D.C. were always memorable. I would go to work with my grandparents and accompany Grandma Sue to the Pentagon, where she met with government officials. I would always be introduced as her granddaughter, Doodlebug. Those trips to the Pentagon seemed to last all day, yet I was content to sit in the cafeteria eating hot donuts and French fries while the adults talked.

Grandma Sue, quite the dresser, wore fancy clothes. During my visits, each morning I sat next to her on the vanity bench in front of her dressing table absorbing each step of her makeup ritual. She began by cleaning her face with Pond's facial cream. Next she put on her Merle Norman facial foundation, then eye makeup and face powder that she applied with a powder puff. In place of a brush, she used her little finger to apply bright red lipstick. Her ritual concluded after she placed several drops of *Tweed* perfume behind each ear. *Tweed* was as important to Grandma Sue as her *Jack Daniels* whiskey.

After I became an adult, I often thought about that perfume. Like Grandma Sue, I shopped at Woodruff and Lothrop in D.C., but I never found her Tweed perfume. Ten years ago, while looking through a Vermont Store catalog, I finally found it. I was thrilled to have my very own bottle, but the thrill didn't last long. For some reason, the perfume didn't smell like I remembered it. But today I still possess that bottle of *Tweed* that sits unused on a shelf in my bathroom.

Grandma Sue wore a showstopper outfit each day. I remember her owning a navy blue crepe sheath with colored rhinestones designed to look like a long-stemmed flower that encompassed the entire right front side of the dress. Her outfit included navy blue sheer stockings, dyed satin shoes, and a large matching purse.

I became enamored with her wardrobe.

At home in Ditchley, I had been used to seeing my other Grandma in handmade cotton skirts and white blouses. Her wardrobe had been sparse yet practical. On Sundays when we attended church, she either wore her only suit, a basic navy blue, or one of the few tailored dresses she owned. Grandma's appearance complemented her personality. A strong-minded person, she didn't make a fuss about clothes. Grandma Sue, however, always looked as if she had stepped from a fashion magazine. She appeared vibrant, swanky, and sexy.

Grandma Sue, a very heavy-set woman, had been a well-known customer at the Lane Bryant Store on F Street in Washington, D.C. She once asked me to help her select a leather purse. Enthusiastically I removed purses from all the shelves within my reach and showed them to her, only to have them rejected. Later she said, "Now Doodlebug, I need a purse big enough to hold all of my important things, including my pint of *Jack Daniels*." It was then I began to believe all Grandmothers who lived in the big city carried large purses with a pint of *Jack Daniels*.

During my visits in the summer, our Saturdays were spent at the Rosecroft Raceway in Maryland. We would sit in front of the big picture window in the air-conditioned clubhouse that overlooked the raceway while the crowd of people outside sat on the bleachers.

Grandma Sue placed bets on the horses I selected. During the races, she had the tenacity to turn away from me and open her purse. I assumed she was taking out money to put on the next bet. My favorite number was three, and after I tired of shouting "Come on Fe" I would begin to whine and ask, "When can we visit the horses?" Skipping toward the stables, but always looking back, I'd soon find myself standing in front of a horse stall, where I waited for my grandparents. Once Grandma Sue took a hard fall that resulted in her rolling around on the soft ground. Laughing loudly I said, "Big fat cow falls down." Neither of my grandparents acknowledged my rude remark.

I was adored by both sets of grandparents, and like all grandchildren, I enjoyed being spoiled. Grandma Sue and Grandpa Ted frequently visited me in Ditchley. Whenever Grandma got the telephone call that my other grandparents were coming for the weekend, we all got busy making sure the guest bedroom was presentable, the grass was cut, and there was plenty of food in the house. Finally, after they arrived, Grandma Sue would exit the Ford station wagon carrying many packages and her large purse. Grandpa Ted always seemed to be left behind to struggle with the luggage that eventually he carried upstairs to the bedroom. After giving and receiving hugs, Grandma and I would be invited to gather around the bed to watch Grandma Sue unpack. She always arrived with special gifts for both of us. "Emily, I thought this dress would look nice on you. So go ahead and try it on. Let's see how it fits."

Grandma, not wanting to offend Grandma Sue, would take the dress and disappear into a bedroom.

Later she returned wearing it and, whether or not it looked good, Grandma Sue's comment always would be the same, "The dress looks perfect." Grandma Sue brought other gifts, like stockings and underwear.

On one of her visits, she arrived with an abundance of packages, and instructed Grandpa Ted to take them directly to the kitchen and put them on the table for Grandma to open. She had given Grandma a complete set of *Revere Ware* pans with copper bottoms. Grandma Sue had thought these new pans would replace Grandma's dented aluminum pans. When the weekend ended, Grandma stored the new pans under the counter and brought them out for only special occasions -- visits from Grandma Sue and Grandpa Ted.

When it came to managing money, my Grandmothers were complete opposites, yet both were generous individuals. During a Thanksgiving visit, Grandma Sue asked if we had any neighbors in need of food. Grandma spoke about a family on Route 200 who lived in an old farmhouse that looked as if it were falling down. She had seen the children standing at the end of the lane in cold weather without coats as they waited for the school bus. Grandma Sue reached into her big purse and took out her checkbook.

Two days before Christmas we went grocery shopping. We got home late, and Grandma instructed me to leave the groceries in the car. It had gotten dark by the time we finished supper. Grandma, who had left the kitchen before removing the dishes from the table, returned wearing her coat and holding her purse. "Baby, get your coat. We've got an errand to take care of."

I knew when to ask questions, and this was not one of those times. We got in the car, and Grandma turned on the headlights as we headed towards Route 200. We hadn't travelled far when Grandma slowed down the car and turned into a dirt lane. Our car lights shone on the house in the distance. In the window was a lighted candle.

After we arrived in front of the house, Grandma cut off the car lights and engine and instructed me not to get out. We had a full moon that night, and sitting there in the cold, I watched Grandma lift the bags of groceries, reach through the screenless door hanging by one hinge, and set her purchases on the porch.

No words were spoken. I understood what she had done, but I didn't understand why she had chosen to handle it that way.

So I asked, "Grandma, Why didn't you knock on the door? You know someone was home because of the burning candle in the window."

"No one wants others to know when they are down on their luck. It's just best we perform our deeds in silence."

I never forgot that night, and often I have wondered how that family felt, finding bags of groceries left on their porch by strangers.

6

SUNDAYS

**Photo 7 - Grace Chapel
Kilmarnock, Virginia**

The cemetery in back of Grace Episcopal Church is where my great-grandmother, grandfather, grandmother, mother, and father are buried. The "Grace Chapel," formerly known as Grace Church, is where my religion began. Grace Chapel is where I was christened. I was confirmed at Christ Church and in 1967 married at Grace Church.

Grace Chapel today sits in back of the existing Grace Church on South Main Street in Kilmarnock. My grandfather Carter Keane, a long-time member of the vestry, oversaw the building of the new Grace Church sometime during the late 1950s.

During my childhood, if you went to church, you dressed up. On Saturday, Grandma would start to plan what I would wear the next morning. The outfit would include white gloves, a hat, and at age eleven after my confirmation, I carried my personal prayer book.

I could skip Sunday school if I promised to sit still during the church service.

My two cousins, Eddie and Richard, who lived with us, carried the cross in church on Sundays. Therefore, we usually arrived early at church. Always a nuisance, my cousins did their very best to stay clear of me for fear I would see something they had done and squeal on them to Grandma and Granddaddy. The old black Buick slowly crept up the road on Sunday mornings with Granddaddy driving, Grandma sitting on the passenger side, and, if I could make it happen, me sitting in the back between Eddie and Richard.

It was hard for me to be good during the long service held in Grace Chapel. Two long-time church members, Hurst Harvey and Victor Richardson, routinely served as ushers and always sat in the back row of the chapel. I sat between my grandparents on the row in front of them. Hurst and Victor liked to try and get me in trouble. They would "discreetly" pull on the ends of my hair during the service. I never understood why Grandma and Granddaddy didn't say something to them. It seemed as if it was expected that I endure their torture as a condition for skipping Sunday school. I shook my head when I felt their fingers on my hair. I could see, from the corner of my eye, their delight when Grandma gave me a stern look that said, "You better sit still." But I must have liked their attention, because after the service I always gave them a hug before leaving church.

Easter at Grace Chapel

The Easter season became my favorite religious holiday. The church altar, decorated in colors of rich purple and gold, created a feeling of intensity, as if surrounded by mystery. Inside the silent walls I felt safe yet full of anticipation that something special would soon be happening.

Photo 8   Mama and me on Easter Sunday

On Easter Sunday, a wooden cross would be placed on the front lawn of the church. It was the custom for children to participate in pinning fresh flowers to the cross on Palm Sunday. The plain painted cross underwent an immediate transformation masked by fresh spring flowers that brought it to life.

On the day before Easter Sunday, a church Easter egg hunt always took place. It became a tradition that my friend Bobbi, a member of Bluff Point Methodist Church, would attend my egg hunt, and then I would attend hers

Photo 9   Decorating the wooden cross with flowers at Easter

At age nine, tired of not winning the annual prize, a large decorated chocolate egg, I decided there would be an easy way to win. After each of us had gathered our eggs, I convinced Bobbi to add her eggs to my basket. Proudly I stepped forward to the lady who awarded the prize. She had a curious look on her face, but without saying anything she counted my eggs. Of course I won the egg. However, I knew I had done something wrong. On the way back to Bobbi's house we did not talk. We took our prize egg into the kitchen, and I watched Bobbi remove the wax paper and cut two slices.

"Here. You take this piece."

There I stood with the sticky slice of egg in my hand. I nibbled at it. Bobbi took her slice and tasted it.

"This is terrible. I don't want it."

"I agree."

I followed Bobbi to the trashcan, where we threw away our prize egg.

Christ Church

Photo 10 - Christ Church

We attended Grace Chapel (later replaced by Grace Church) for three seasons and went to Christ Church in the summer.

All summer services were held at Christ Church. At Christ Church, our family sat in the "Carter" pew.

Upon arrival, if summer visitors had happened to invade our turf, no matter how many other pews were available Granddaddy boldly led us into the family pew. Sometimes the space became so tight, I had to sit on Grandma's lap through the entire service. Christ Church.

Each June a confirmation service would take place at Christ Church. The Bishop came and conducted the service. Homecoming Sunday also happened that day. Most families would arrive with a card table, chairs, a tablecloth, silverware, cloth napkins, and a picnic basket to share. Grandma always brought fried chicken, deviled eggs, and a homemade yellow layer cake with hardened chocolate boiled icing. Before going into church we set up the tables and chairs, everyone vying for a shady spot close to the desserts.

We always arrived early. Grandma especially enjoyed being a part of the women's group that stayed outside during the service and oversaw setting out the food.

The confirmation service lasted a long time. Before "Amen" echoed throughout the church, everyone left and quickly moved towards the tables covered in food, where a line began to form. White sheets covered the tables that had been made of saw horses and plywood, set up to form a square. Inside the square, the church ladies stood, grouped in front of a particular food section, such as the desserts, and made sure the pies, cakes and cobblers had been cut and proper serving utensil were present. The men took care of overseeing the sweetened iced tea that had been stored in five-gallon milk cans and kept in the back of a pickup truck. The food always seemed to taste better than anything served at home.

> *Once we returned home, Grandma's picnic basket seemed to be a lot heavier. A closer look inside revealed the truth--finding it filled with a variety of leftover desserts. All week we continued to enjoy Homecoming.*

7

Outdoor Play

Photo 11   Mama and me in 1953

Our playground was the outdoors. In winter we ice skated on Norris' Pond and went sledding on Porter's Hill. In the summer, we spent the day at the Tidewater Foundation (an outdoor recreation facility) and sailed from Indian Creek Yacht and Country Club. On Saturday night we danced until midnight at White Stone Beach. Opportunities like these no longer exist. Change washed them away.

The seasonal Sears and Roebuck mail order catalogs provided hours of indoor play. We cut out color pictures and glued them to cardboard to make paper dolls. We lined the interior of cardboard boxes with pictures of furniture and called them dollhouses.

Although inside play was fun, the most memorable fun was during the winter and summer seasons. Our winters here in The Neck were cold. There was plenty of snow, too. We would ride sleighs and ice skate.

Norris' Pond, north of Kilmarnock on Route 3, was where we skated. When the night skating began, my granddaddy, Carter Keane, ordered ice skates for both me and my best friend Bobbi Gaskins. With skates in hand, we were ready to join our school friends on the ice. I dressed warmly in my flannel-lined jeans, a heavy coat, and layers of wool socks, wool gloves, scarf, and hat. Even so, I got cold on the ice. My fingers and toes grew numb, but that didn't diminish my enthusiasm to ice skate.

I was told that as long as we heard the sound of the ice cracking, it was safe to skate. I hesitated in believing that, but after all I was a child; therefore I listened to adults. After a good freeze, the local Kilmarnock Fire Department brought a tanker truck to the pond and sprayed the pond with water to smooth the surface.

Not many adults skated, but Granddaddy always joined us kids out on the ice. Those on shore watched and kept the fire roaring by adding windfall and old tires. At the edge of the pond a heavy rope was kept, just in case someone fell in. Precaution prevailed, and there were no accidents.

There were motionless moments on the ice when we stood and watched Mr. Luther Chipwell skate. This elderly man entertained everyone with his figure eights and graceful backward skating. The smile on his face said it all. Mr. Chipwell loved to skate and to help those of us who didn't skate well.

◦≋◦

Sledding was another winter activity. On Route 200 just outside of Kilmarnock, there was a big farm we called Porter's Farm. It had a huge hill that faced Bluff Point Road. Now sixty years later, the hill no longer seems huge.

Mr. Henderson Porter owned the farm. He was a farmer who enjoyed crocheting table place mats and doilies. In the evenings, the locals sat on their front porches, rocked, talked, and discussed Mr. Porter's status of being a "forever bachelor." However, my first and second grade teacher, Miss Eleanora Haynie, changed that status.

Everyone assumed the gentle, pleasant Miss Haynie, who devoted her entire life to teaching and church, had no time for other activities. When there was news that Miss Haynie accompanied Mr. Porter on Sunday drives, the community was shocked. After years of Mr. Porter courting Miss Haynie, the Porter farm acquired a Mrs. Porter.

Photo 12 - Porter's Hill
Our favorite sledding site

Whenever we had a heavy snow, Bobbi and I did lots of begging for her parents or my grandparents to take us to Porter's Hill and to drop us off to go sledding. On one particular day I had gone to the hill alone. The bright sun beat down on the snow while footsteps smashed against the crusty surface, creating a loud crunching sound. I walked towards a group of boys standing at the edge of the hill who were jumping up and down. I was not sure if they were cold, excited, or scared. I chose to ignore them as I passed by.

I lifted my Western Flyer sled and brushed the loose snow from the runners. Carefully I placed the sled on the snow, facing down hill. I jumped on and, using the weight of my body, kicked with my feet to make it move. The wind blew across my face as I sped down the hill. I tightly held on with my hands, ready to change direction should anyone get in the way. Suddenly it was over. The ride had ended too soon, yet I was still energized and couldn't wait to reach the top of the hill so that I could do it all over again.

In the late afternoon, I saw Grandma's car parked on Bluff Point Road on the other side of the fence. It was time for me to go home. Hurriedly I jumped on my sled and started down the hill. I looked back and saw a loose bull headed my way. When I got to the bottom, my sled hit a fence post. I scrambled to get over the fence, leaving behind my sled and one white boot in the snow. Grandma retrieved both the sled and the boot. Cold and upset by having been chased by a bull, I quickly opened the door and climbed in to Grandma's car.

When the deep snows came, the most fun we had was nighttime sledding on Porter's Hill, where a big bonfire helped warm my numb fingers and toes. Someone in the community owned a wooden bobsled that seated six people. At first everyone was enthusiastic and wanted to ride on it. But after one downhill run, our enthusiasm weakened when it came time to drag the heavy wooden sled back up the hill. After winter ended, our thoughts turned to summer and the end of school.

During the summer, we enjoyed the Tidewater Recreation Facility, where Bobbi and I sailed from Indian Creek Yacht and Country Club, swam, and danced at White Stone Beach on Saturday night. The Kilmarnock White Stone Rotary Club had bought land in Fleets Bay and built The Tidewater Foundation, a family summer outdoor recreation facility located on Indian Creek. Granddaddy installed the saltwater pool. There was also a wading pool, a beautiful wooded picnic area, a children's playground with swings, and bathhouses. The cost for the family season ticket was $25.00. It was quite a distance from the parking lot to the facility. To get there we walked on a dirt path through the woods and over the wooden bridge that had been built by a local Boy Scout troop. At night the isolated parking lot, surrounded by woods, transitioned into the local "Lover's Lane."

Photo 13 - Bobbi and me on her front porch. Hard to believe a few years later we would trade our bare feet for ball gowns.

As a fundraiser event, the Rotarians sold cement-casted footprints. Each Rotarian was asked to pay $100 to have the footprint of his or her grandchild and the child's name put on display at the facility. Our footprints were taken at the dedication ceremony. The children lined up according to age, beginning with the youngest child at the front of the line. One by one with an adult on each side, we stepped forward and placed a foot on the wet cement.

Someone said, "Get ready and we'll lift you up."

Granddaddy grabbed my ankle and held my foot firmly in place. After my foot was lifted from the cement, I plunked it into a bucket of water. I had been reassured the excess cement would easily come off. Several weeks later, I still had one gray-colored foot.

All summer long my friend Bobbi and I sailed from the *Indian Creek Yacht and Country Club* to the *Tidewater Foundation* recreational facility. Our families met us there to swim and to share a picnic of fried chicken, deviled eggs, homemade sweet cucumber pickles, and ice-cold watermelon.

The facility closed, and the property was sold. Today houses rest on the property that once was the *Tidewater Foundation*.

By the time I graduated from high school, the use of the recreation facility was on the decline.

Photo 14 - Photograph of White Stone Beach

White Stone Beach was another popular hot spot in the summer. We took swimming lessons in the river and danced in the pavilion on Saturday nights.

The Red Cross held swimming lessons for children in the community. The swimming instructor, Captain Pleasants, stood in the water ready to catch any child brave enough to jump off the high pier or dive from the two-by-four wooden plank diving board. A net used to keep sea nettles out blocked off a large area in the water, but some still got in.

At the White Stone Beach Hotel, rooms and a cottage were available to rent. Both locals and the out-of town guests who stayed there patronized the dining room.

The public had access, free of charge, to use the beach for picnics and sun bathing. On any hot day, an ice cream cone bought from inside the pavilion at the soda fountain provided much welcomed relief from the heat.

Amy and Gilbert Culver owned the facility. Under the roof overhang of the pavilion, white rocking chairs faced out into the Rappahannock River. Mrs. Culver, Gilbert's mother, was a fixture at White Stone Beach. She used to sit and rock for hours while watching the active children who swam in the river or played on the beach. Other times she seemed interested in the young people who came by boat from both sides of the Rappahannock River and tied up at the pier to join the Saturday night dance.

On Saturday nights, a crowd of teenagers lined up and waited outside. Mr. Culver collected a $5.00-per-person admission charge and stamped each person's hand so that people could freely go in and out of the pavilion. While there was no dress code, the majority of the people wore white Bermuda shorts, madras blouses or shirts, and Weegan loafers without socks. Many of us were too young to buy beer. But the guys always had a supply of cold beer or a five-gallon container of Purple Passion (grape juice and sloe gin) in the trunk of the car. As the night heated up, there were frequent trips to the parking lot. While the music flowed from inside the pavilion, some people spread blankets down on the sand beach, and a party began. The party was short-lived, because the music called. We went to White Stone Beach to dance and to see who was dating whom.

Around 8:30 p.m. a van would arrive with the musicians, a group known as the *Dynatones,* an all-black male band. They wore red blazers, ties, white shirts, and white pants. Sometime during the night and more than once, they played the song *Jeremiah was a Bullfrog.* Everyone pushed to get onto the crowded floor. We danced, sang, and yelled. With arms held high and fingers dancing in the air, beads of body sweat rolled from our foreheads. Heads bobbed, and with a low swinging motion like the pendulum on a clock, our butts touched. The music was in control. When the band stopped playing at midnight, it was time to go home.

In the parking lot a stuck car rested in the sand. Guys banded together in an attempt to free it. A failed rescue meant the guy had drunk too much Purple Passion. So whoever needed a ride was driven home. What fun we had! Years later White Stone closed. The property was sold. There is no public access to the beach today.

I continue to replay those memories -- all of the summers and winters, when we lived outdoors and enjoyed unorganized activities, absent from electronic games and cell phones. It was a time when kids developed their imaginations and enjoyed building lifetime relationships with their friends.

Photo 15 Nellerie Johnson and me at the Ditchley Packing Company

8

GROWING UP IN THE SEAFOOD BUSINESS

Photo 16   Fuggie and me
He was part of the seafood business.

My grandfather owned and operated the Ditchley Packing Company in the 1950s. During most of the year, a hub of activities transpired when local watermen arrived by boat to sell fish, crabs, and oysters. During the week I would visit the plant and socialize with my friends, the workers, and the watermen.

The men workers, Nellerie Johnson, Walter Harris, and Roamie and Wallace Carter, were unofficially tasked to look out for "Little Gwen." Nothing moves slowly in the seafood business, so when wheelbarrows loaded with oysters were transported from the dock to the plant, these men stood ready to push me aside and keep me from being run over.

The plant was built on large creosote pilings close to the shoreline and could easily be identified by the enormous oyster shell pile located at the back door. To a small child aged five, the white mountain had been just a toy. Sometimes I pretended to be an aerial artist, trying to balance myself as I walked the board planks uphill to reach my mountaintop. The size of the oyster shell pile decreased at the end of the season when the shells were moved by barge to my grandfather's leased oyster ground in the bay.

In the state of Virginia, oyster ground is leased by the acre to private citizens who then are required to periodically re-seed it. For generations some families have continued to lease the same oyster ground. Our oyster ground, which consisted of several parcels totaling twenty-one acres, first had been leased to my great-grandmother Cora Lee Keane, who passed it on to my grandfather, and then I inherited it.

Inside the plant, neighborhood ladies sat on stools shucking oysters, picking crabs, or cutting up fish. Cans of oysters later would be packed in wooden fish boxes and covered with ice before being transported by truck to a faraway place called Washington, D. C. Ditchley Packing Company all year round had been a major part of my play world.

Fuggie, my big collie-like dog, would walk with me to the plant. Anxious to get there, he trotted ahead, while I, walking barefoot, lagged behind, trying to avoid the sharp-edged oyster shells that covered our dirt lane. Fuggie had acquired a taste for the fresh raw oysters fed to him by the workers.

In the summer, Fuggie lay on the cool cement floor under the workers' stainless steel cutting table and slept, while I, resting my head on his stomach, examined our surroundings. Inside the dark plant, it would be so hot that the women workers, sitting on stools, pulled up their dresses and exposed their bare legs. We had no electric fans or air conditioning. At supper I once asked Grandma, "Why doesn't Mrs. Mitchell wear panties?" She immediately responded with the question, "How do you know she doesn't wear panties?" After my confession, I had to listen to a lecture on good manners.

On most days there would be little excitement at the plant, unless Mr. Gresham, the seafood inspector, arrived unannounced. Whenever someone spotted his car in the neighborhood, my grandfather would receive a call giving him a heads up.

Everyone, including me, feared Mr. Gresham. I still can visualize that fat little man driving a gray coupe as he sped down our lane, stirring up a trail of dust. Before he could leave his car, he had to free his belly, which rested against the steering wheel. Once standing, Mr. Gresham would try to balance his disproportioned body before walking around to the passenger side and picking up the gray felt derby he wore all year round. The hat, too small for his head, forced strands of his straggly white hair to stick out, making him look like Charlie Chaplin minus a moustache.

Mr. Gresham, an unattractive man, didn't like children or animals. I had been cautioned there would be big trouble if he ever found dog hair near the seafood or if he thought water had been used to blow up the oysters to make them appear fat.

No dogs or cats were allowed inside the plant. Whenever Mr. Gresham arrived, Fuggie and I escaped through the back door. We had our favorite hiding place under the plant, where we would sit behind a piling, forced to inhale the stinky smells of dead seaweed, fish, and crabs. After Mr. Gresham left, we returned inside so that Fuggie could receive his reward, a pan of freshly shucked oysters, compliments from the ladies.

If things had gone well, Granddaddy would walk me over to the plant's convenience store, and give me a Dixie cup of chocolate ice cream he had removed from the freezer. Outside the store, I would sit on the cement stoop and, using a flat piece of thin wood shaped like a spoon, eat my ice cream.

I always tried to be the first person on the dock to greet the watermen and examine the unusual creatures they might have caught in their nets. Sometimes they brought in sea turtles, but the most exotic creature I ever saw was a sea horse. I put it in an open Mason jar filled with creek water and tied it to a dock piling. All day I kept a check on it, lifting the jar to watch the little creature bob up and down. The next morning my sea horse was gone. It swam away during high tide.

On most days I visited with the watermen aboard their boats and ate the cookies they offered me from their lunch pails. I never tired of sitting on boat decks talking to the men or watching the rusty wire baskets loaded with fresh seafood being hoisted up to the dock and emptied into wheelbarrows.

The high-standing dock became more than just a place to sell and off-load seafood. I used to jump from that dock and swim.

Once, after I tried to swim away from the dock, my left ankle touched a piling and brushed against the sharp edge of a barnacle. Later at home I tried to disguise the deep wound by wearing a sock.

Grandma, of course, discovered my injury and called for Dr. Gravatt. When he came to our door, I ran upstairs and hid under the tester bed. He earned his exercise that day when forced to climb under the bed and give me a tetanus shot.

More than fifty years later, I still have the scar and the memory.

In autumn, fewer boats came to the dock, so I entertained myself by poling a skiff around the shore using a crab net to pry lose big oysters from the mud, oysters my grandmother would later shuck and serve at supper. We survived on seafood.

When I became a young adult and left the Northern Neck, many years passed before I ever selected seafood from a menu. I had eaten enough seafood during my childhood. But now, older and wiser, I love seafood as much as any other food group.

9

CAPTAIN PRUETT

Photo 17 Cherry Tree in the front yard of my home in Ditchley, Virginia

Early on a summer morning, as sparkles created by the sun danced on the water and a breeze filled the air, my grandfather Carter Keane and I got in a skiff and motored from our dock to the "Buy Boat" anchored at the edge of the bay and Dividing Creek. Local crabbers surrounded the Buy Boat to offload and sell their morning catch. Capt'n Pruett waved as I handed the deckhand our line. For us, the crab season had started now that Capt'n Pruett had arrived.

For the past several years, at the beginning of each crab season, Capt'n Pruett left his home on Tangier Island to work on the mainland. For the next three months at the Ditchley Packing Company, he would be in charge of the process to oversee the transformation that produced soft-shelled crabs. He ensured the live crabs would be properly packed in wet seaweed to survive the truck ride to Washington, D.C. Hours later, well-dressed diners would savor each bite of the freshly prepared soft-shelled crabs served at the prominent Flagship Restaurant owned by my grandfather's first cousin, Daisy Mattingly.

Capt'n Pruett had been described as a "closet drinker," until he got drunk. Grandma and I were seated in the flower garden enjoying our ice cream when we were interrupted by the sound of a truck engine coming from the direction of the plant. Granddaddy hadn't been home that day, so we abandoned our ice cream and set out to identify the driver of the truck.

The truck swayed as it moved along the edge of the bank. Behind the wheel sat Capt'n Pruett. Grandma placed two fingers in her mouth and gave a "you are in trouble now" whistle. Capt'n Pruett, all liquored up, turned the truck around and headed right for us. We knew he didn't know how to drive because, at that time, Tangier Island did not have any cars. As he drove past us, he yelled, "Mrs. Keane, I'm a-going home! I'm a driving right durn back to Tangier."

Grandma ran after the truck and, as he made another circle, the engine cut off. She went over to the old truck and delivered Capt'n Pruett his well-deserved lecture on safety, the use of someone's personal property without permission, and the evils of excessive drinking. Capt'n Pruett cried! "I didn't mean to do no harm. I'm just so darn homesick."

Grandma, being sympathetic, convinced him to go back to the crab shack and take a nap. She also invited him to supper the next night.

At 5:00 o'clock sharp the next evening, Capt'n Pruett showed up at our back door. While he sat at the table with a plate full of food, the conversation began.

"Mrs. Keane, you sure do have a lot of cherries on those trees in your front yard. I wondered if you ever make any cherry wine?"

That was how Capt'n Pruett got permission to pick the cherries and got Grandma's recipe for cherry wine. The next morning, when he had finished his chores, he climbed up a ladder with bucket in hand and picked cherries.

Later that night, as Grandma and I sat on the porch, loud noises erupted. It sounded as if a shotgun had been fired. Grandma jumped from her rocker and, with me right behind her, we followed the sound. From the top of the bank, we could look down and see the tar-papered crab shack that rested on pilings in the water, surrounded by a dock. With all of the outside lights turned on, we spotted the barrel of a gun propped up in the open window. Grandma hollered, "Capt'n Pruett, are you all right?"

We waited and hoped he would call back.

He yelled, "I am okay, but I sure got a mess on my hands."

Grandma told him we were coming down.

Once inside the shack, we found ourselves walking through a thick, sticky substance, the remainder of the cherry wine. The wine explosion had reached the walls, which were covered in starburst patterns of purplish liquid. Even Capt'n Pruett's mattress had been soaked in wine and covered in sharp pieces of broken glass.

What did you do?" Grandma asked.

"I made the wine, just like you told me. Then I screwed on the tops of the jars and went to bed when my Gawd, Mrs. Keane, suddenly I heard what I thought was a shot, which made me jump from my bed and take cover. I then grabbed this shotgun, 'cause I just knew someone had shot at me. It wasn't until I heard you call that I realized my wine had blown up."

"Capt'n Pruett, your wine blew up because you put tight lids on the hot jars."

For years thereafter, during our summer evenings spent on the porch, Grandma would rock and repeat her favorite story of Capt'n Pruett's wine explosion.

10

THE CURRY FAMILY

Photo 18   Lonnie and Minnie Curry

Lonnie and Minnie Curry raised nineteen children in their well kept home, located inland on Route 669 just before the intersection to the Ditchley glades. Lonnie, a self-employed waterman, sold his oysters and crabs to my grandfather Carter Keane. Kindness to thy neighbor had been a value that ran deep in the Curry family.

The cool air and a drop in the water temperature never kept us from going out on the creek, especially on a pretty day. One chilly November day I stood on the bow of the skiff with Grandma seated in the stern as I poled around the shore.

Grandma, who had been leaning over the side of the skiff, put her hand down deep into the cold water and lifted oysters from the mud bottom. These oysters would soon be our supper.

"Watch those low limbs hanging over the water," she cautioned me, a nine-year-old child who paid no attention to the warning.

"Just duck your head," I thought. Then I heard the whoosh, and something hit the water. I feared what I would see as I turned around. Grandma's hairnet had gotten caught on a tiny tree branch, and she had been pulled overboard. I began yelling and almost fell overboard myself as I tried to turn the skiff around to rescue her.

The current moved my skiff away from Grandma and out into the middle of the creek. In the distance I saw a figure-- someone aboard a workboat dressed in yellow oilskins, tonging for oysters. He had heard my scream and wasted no time starting up his engine. While my skiff aimlessly moved further out into the creek, I watched him make the rescue. He lifted Grandma from the water and placed her on the floor of his boat before coming in my direction.

"Hand me your line," he shouted.

I threw him the line, but missed. Two more attempts, and finally it reached his boat. I felt helpless and prayed silently for Grandma, while the boat plowed through the water and headed towards my grandfather's dock. Once there I stood by

Grandma's side, watching her being lifted from the boat and hoisted up to the dock.

She appeared to be warm, wrapped up in an old boat blanket. Lucky for us, Mr. Lonnie Curry had been there to help and had responded quickly. I told this story to Joe Curry, a local well-respected businessman, civic leader, and a son of the late Lonnie and Minnie Curry. In turn, he told me a story about my grandfather when he had been the Manager of the East Coast Utility Company and had brought the first electric line to Ditchley. Joe described the main transformer in Ditchley as not being far from his family's house, and he said my grandfather had authorized an "unofficial" hook-up to their home. The Curry's then became the first black family in Ditchley to have electricity.

The Curry family, like most families who lived in the inland part of Ditchley, were trusted, well-respected people. Segregation existed, but when it came to helping neighbors, my community had been colorless.

11

ELEMENTARY SCHOOL DAYS

Photo 19   Wicomico Elementary School
Wicomico Church, Virginia

A major change occurred for me when it was time to begin the third grade. The old Kilmarnock School no longer accepted elementary school students. I would be forced to attend Wicomico Elementary School, where new experiences and new friends would write another chapter in my life.

On the first day of school, accompanied by Grandma, I walked down the long hallway of pink-painted walls. The floor, a brown rubber tile, was slippery. Trying not to fall, we continued to search for a door marked "Third Grade." Once we got inside the room, Mrs. Lewis, the teacher, said I had to sit down and that Grandma should leave. The room was filled with old wooden desks attached to chairs. At the upper right-hand corner of the desk, there was a hole for a bottle of ink. I am left-handed.

The tall, slim, gray-haired Mrs. Beatrice Lewis stood in front of the room. She wore a long-sleeved, high-collared white blouse and a gray-colored, gored skirt with a black belt. Her black, laced-up shoes looked very "old maid- like." She appeared to be stern in nature; yet, as I would later learn, she loved her children, and she loved to teach. Science was her favorite subject.

Mrs. Lewis lived within a few miles of this small community and knew the parents of the children she taught. During cold weather, some children came to school without a coat. There were also children in need of shoes. Several times I witnessed Mrs. Lewis provide those necessities to her children, yet she always had been careful never to draw attention to her acts of kindness. Mrs. Lewis became my teacher in the third, fourth, fifth, and seventh grades.

**Photo 20 - Our Gang - Rudy Lester, Teresa Blevins, Ann Thorndike, Peggy Fuller and me
1961**

In the third grade, I became close friends with my desk mate, Peggy (Peg) Fuller. We weren't bad little girls, but we were mischievous. I discovered my natural gift of leadership skills. Before the school year ended, I had become the leader of our group of five: four girls, and one boy, Rudy Lester, who later, as a young adult, became the first soldier in Northumberland County to die in the Viet Nam War.

At recess, the five of us gathered outside and, using our imaginations, created characters for our spontaneous plays. Sometimes we just played games, like hide-and-seek or hopscotch. Peg and I spent many weekends together during the school year. In the summer, we expanded the length of our visits to each other's houses.

Peg's mom, Mrs. Fuller, and Grandma were good sports who put up with our schemes. Often when Peg's mom took me home, I would ask Grandma if Peg could spend the weekend. Her reply never varied. "Yes, if Mrs. Fuller doesn't mind." Mrs. Fuller would speak to Peg and say, "Well, you don't have any clothes." Then Peg and I would open up the car trunk and show them the suitcase.

Both Grandma and Mrs. Fuller pretended to be surprised.

I don't recall us doing anything at my house that got us into trouble. But at Peg's house there were more temptations. She had an older brother Arthur (Art), whose life we tried to make miserable. I decided Arthur should join us one summer night after their parents had gone to bed. We climbed out the upstairs window and went down a ladder we had placed there earlier in the day. Peg and I, dressed in our shortie pajamas, ran towards the woods shouting, as Arthur ran after us. Just as we crossed the open field, a lit cigarette caught our attention. Mr. Fuller sat on the front steps smoking. The three of us then tried to hide as we crouched down closer to the ground. After what seemed forever, he finally called out, "Okay kids, it's time to come inside." We had failed to notice the light from the full moon. The next morning at breakfast Mr. Fuller made no mention of the previous night.

When we were older, Peg, Arthur, and I decided to imitate the adults and celebrate New Year's Eve. We associated champagne with New Year's Eve parties. But because we had no champagne, we concocted our own drink. First we found an empty jar that smelled of peanut butter. Arthur offered up a stale can of beer he had found near Mr. Northern's pier. We poured the beer in the jar, added a raw egg, and shook it well. Then Peg and I told Arthur he had to be the first to taste the drink. Being the oldest, he agreed that he should go first. It must have tasted awful, because Arthur spit out the drink, which went everywhere in the kitchen. We knew we had to clean it up, but we didn't want to wake up Mr. and Mrs. Fuller. Peg took an aluminum saucepan off the stove. We filled it with water and added some laundry soap. Under the cabinet we found an old rag. After we washed up everything, we set the pan back on the stove. It was too late to celebrate, so we just went to bed.

The next morning when we got to the breakfast table, Mrs. Fuller served us oatmeal from the aluminum pan we had used earlier to clean up the kitchen. She mentioned being concerned because none of us seemed hungry.

After all, the three of us had always loved oatmeal.

When Peg and I visited each other's houses, we spent most of our time outside. There were no worries about child molesters. Children our age played freely and away from parental sight. We knew how long we could be gone. We knew how far we could travel. And no one had to threaten us, because we just knew we had better not break the rules. Peg had a little wooden skiff we used to row across the creek. On the way over, if we saw a crab pot we would empty it and at the end of the day we steamed the crabs. We never thought that taking the crabs had been wrong; after all, the pot had been found in the creek, and everyone owned the creek.

After pulling the boat up on the sand beach we would climb the high clay cliffs that rose above the sand beach, grab a vine, and swing down into the water. Later, if we had enough time and money, we rowed over to Glebe Point to buy a Coke and penny candy from Mrs. Cockrell's store.

Long before the arrival of spring, high school girls in the community talked about the upcoming high school proms. Peg and I both wanted to see what had been causing so much excitement. We convinced her mom to drive us to Kilmarnock where the four of us, Arthur included, sat in their pink and black Studebaker outside of the Kilmarnock High School. From the car we had a good view of the girls dressed in rainbow-colored gowns and their dates wearing white dinner jackets as they walked up to the doors of the school. We thought the full-skirted strapless gowns made of layered netting were beautiful. After we returned home that night, Peg and I danced in the front yard, pretending to be those pretty girls in prom dresses.

In May, we became the excited ones as our school prepared for the big May Day event. Each class participated in the theme celebration. One year our class dressed up as pioneers. Mr. Hatton, who lived close by, owned an old covered wagon he put in the schoolyard. When the music began, the girls, dressed in colonial dresses and bonnets, along with the boys, who wore vests, short pants, and knee socks, exited the wagon. We formed two circles and square danced. Another year the girls dressed up as the New York City "Rockettes." We wore blue vests, full-circled blue skirts lined in red, and crinolines with borders of red lace. After the boys sang several patriotic songs, the girls performed the "can-can." Another year, both the boys and the girls dressed up in green plaid kilts. We crossed swords on the ground and danced a Scottish jig. At the end of each year's performance, we danced around the Maypoles, weaving the long pastel ribbons. That evening, after the baseball games had ended and everyone was full from eating hot dogs, a talent show was held in the auditorium.

Photo 21   Bobbi and me in the May Day Variety Show
Wicomico Elementary School

Bobbi Gaskins and I once entered that talent show. For weeks, we practiced our tap dance. Both of us had previously attended the local annual Lion's Club Minstrel Show, where everyone in the show put black grease paint on his or her face. We modeled ourselves after that show and took the first prize.

12

The Child Sailors

**Photo 22   Sailboat Race
Indian Creek**

I sat in Grandma's lap as she rocked and retold the family sailing stories. She crewed for both my grandfather and my father, who were serious sailors in World War II. As members of the local Rappahannock River Yacht Club in Irvington, Virginia, they participated in weekend sailing races. My grandmother used to say that while most everyone kept their competitive spirits in tack, the pranksters who came from the Hampton, Newport News, and Norfolk sailing clubs were the fiercest competitors.

Grandma's stories convinced me sailing must be great fun and something I did not want to miss. For years, I begged Granddaddy for a sailboat. Finally, when I was 11, he bought me an eleven-foot wooden Penguin Class sailboat. It became a memorable day when we went to Deltaville and picked up my baby blue sailboat.

This had not been just any old boat!

This boat had been a champion on the bay. For several years it had won every race in its class. I was so proud to own such a boat, and I wanted to give it a meaningful name. Otherwise, I could never have bonded with it.

I learned from Granddaddy that "trimming the sail," which is almost an art, had been a term sailors use to describe a full sail. It occurs when the boat's weight is properly balanced. With a good wind, the sailboat can be made to lean on one side close to the water's edge, almost touching, but not taking in any water. Thus, I decided to name the boat *Cuddle-Up*.

My best friend and neighbor, Bobbi, became just as excited as I was when she learned about the sailboat, and she asked to be my crew. Since neither of us knew anything about sailing, my grandfather, the Commodore of the Sailing Club at our local country club, suggested we take a basic sailing course.

On hot Tuesday nights that summer, along with the other "wanna-be sailors," we sat in a little non-air-conditioned boat shack with beads of sweat rolling from our foreheads as we tried to learn the principles of sailing. I had not been sure what could be worse--sitting in a hot room for hours or being told that we had to demonstrate what we had learned.

Reluctantly, I put on my jeans over my bathing suit. Bobbi and I took the *Cuddle-Up* out into Indian Creek, where we sat rocking the boat back and forth until we had been successful in capsizing it. The moment arrived to remove our jeans and tie a knot in each pants leg. We threw the knotted pants legs over our backs in an effort to inflate them. Success! We had made ourselves life preservers. Under normal conditions, an opportunity to cool off in the creek would always be welcomed, but now we just wanted to avoid being stung by the nettle-infested seawater.

The exercise did not end until we had been successful in taking down the heavy water-soaked sail that lay in the water, up righting the boat, and climbing back aboard.

After weeks of classroom instruction and plenty of hands-on experience, Bobbi and I got called forward and were awarded certificates of completion in Basic Seamanship.

Overly confident, we were anxious to practice our newly learned skills. Sailing became our summertime recreation. Each day either we left from my shore, or I sailed to Bobbi's dock and picked her up. Part of our routine gear included peanut butter and jelly sandwiches, a jug of water, two flotation devices, a bailing scoop, a sponge, and an anchor. We sailed from Prentice Creek to the edge of the bay, as we were forbidden from going out into the bay. However, sometimes temptation won.

Little did we know that Grandma stood at a second floor window with binoculars in hand, watching every "tack" and "about" we did in that little eleven-foot sailboat. Normally we escaped being punished for our misdeeds and received a reminder that sailing was a privilege, not an inherited right.

We might not have known everything about sailing, but we knew the signs of bad weather approaching. We had been raised in families who made their living from the water. Sometimes, though, we barely reached the shore before a driving rain soaked our sails, yet we always arrived home safely before lightning started.

On Labor Day, the end of our first season of sailing, Bobbi and I entered a sail race sponsored by the Sailing Club at the *Indian Creek Yacht and Country Club*. There would be five boats in the race. Four of the boats had already arrived at the club and were being off-loaded when the fifth boat came. It belonged to some newcomers from up-state New York. Their boat, made of that new material called fiberglass, gave it the advantage of being lighter in weight and, in theory, faster.

Bobbi and I immediately recognized the challenge that lay ahead. We knew that keeping a full sail would be important, but we had to make sure the others never used their sails to block out the wind. We also understood the importance of going around the buoys on the assigned course as tightly as we could without hitting one. Hitting a buoy would be an automatic disqualification.

At long last all five racing boats entered Indian Creek, with each of us trying to establish our best starting position. First we sailed up close to the starting line, and I yelled, "about," hoping not to cross the line before the gun went off, as that would be an automatic disqualification. Of course, we had other major concerns--that we never hit a boat while trying to stay on course and keeping our sail full. If our competitive spirit could have been substituted for wind, our sail would have always been full.

BANG! The race started, and we had been in the right position, about a foot from the starting line, headed in the right direction, and with almost a full sail. "Tighten the sheet line," I shouted to Bobbi, and off we went. At first all five boats moved along pretty well.

We quickly approached the first buoy, and being on course I yelled to Bobbi, "We need to tack." She nodded, and I gave the command "about." As we turned, Bobbi slackened the sheet line so that the boom could smoothly transition to the other side of the boat.

Just as I completed bringing the boat about, Bobbi quickly pulled in the sheet line and there we were--the *Cuddle-Up* with a full sail--leaning so close to the water's edge we almost touched it and heading directly towards the course marker.

We sailed diagonally and crossed over in front of the other four boats. Once we had rounded the buoy, we found ourselves in the lead, with a trim sail as we navigated a tight course.

We continued in the lead. As we crossed the finish line, we heard the loud bang of the gun and the announcement from the Committee Boat that the winner had been number 1475. Filled with joy, it's a wonder we didn't throw our hands up and capsize the Cuddle-Up.

We sailed directly to shore, hoping not to do anything stupid that would cause embarrassment, since all eyes had been on us.

We became even more excited when Granddaddy called the Captain, (me) and my crewmember, Bobbi, forward and gave me the trophy.

Afterwards Bobbi asked, "Don't I get a trophy, too?"

"No," I told my best friend. "The Captain outranks the crew."

Our sailing days happened more than fifty years ago, and today we're still best friends.

Photo 23   Fishing Boats

13

THE FISH HUNT

Photo 24   Menhadden Fish Boat docked in Reedville, Virginia

At the turn of the century, Elijah Reed, a man from Brooklyn, Maine, built a six-kettle fish factory in Reedville, Virginia. This Northerner founded the Chesapeake Bay menhaden industry.

The menhaden are small, purplish-black, bony fish, members of the herring family. They are used for making products like cat food, fertilizer, and paint. In the 1950s the menhaden industry had been a major player in our local economy. Everyone knew someone connected to the industry: a fish boat captain, his wife, or a local grocery supplier that "grubbed up" the boat.

The industry not only affected the economy, it influenced how people were looked upon in the community.

As a naïve child growing up in the 1950s, I was complacent with life and my surroundings. At home the word integration, like a contagious disease, was never discussed. I became an adult before I learned the truth about the Civil War. In the fourth grade, when we studied Virginia history, a discussion of the Civil War had been limited to the great battles fought and the generals who led the battles. Being a Southerner, I assumed Northerners must be bad people who wanted us to give up our Confederacy, whatever that was. In my world, the black people around here lived in their own communities, physically and socially separate from white families.

When I began to write my memories of growing up in rural Virginia, I discovered separatism also existed within the commercial fishing industry. During the early days of menhaden fishing, manual labor had been a necessity. The all-black crews existed as early as 1915, and up to the 1950s most of the crewmembers were entirely black, the exceptions being the captain, pilot, mate, and chief engineer.

Unfortunately, crews who had payroll problems were not welcomed at factory offices. The captains were responsible for resolving the crews pay issues. However, in the early 1950s, after black crewmembers advanced to the position of mate, they became the conduit between the rest of the crew and the factory offices. This freed up the captains so they could focus on the fishing operations aboard the vessels. The captains hired their own crews and welcomed back those who chose to return the next season. It would be financially rewarding for a crewmember to work for the captain of the "high boat" (number one boat on the bay for the fish season). Although the captain got paid a higher wage than the crew, pay was based on the volume of fish caught.

A crewmember that signed on at the beginning of the season did not get paid unless his boat caught fish. A portion of each paycheck would be withheld until the end of the season. If a crewmember quit before the season ended, he lost his entire back pay. Grub bills would be deducted from the crews' wages, and if the fishing season had been poor, they could end up owing the factory.

Aboard the fish boat, the captain's position was one of power. He decided where to tie up the boat at night and whether or not to return to the factory located in the community of Fleeton. The captain understood navigation. There were no computers to rely on and no GPSs. He knew how to read his instruments and track the weather, tides, and currents.

Before a man could become a menhaden boat captain, he earned his living as a waterman. A waterman knew how to spot fish. He could recognize a subtle movement in the water's surface, whips or changes in surface color, or the slightly different hue on distant waters, all indicators that fish were present. The crews, proud of their captain's knowledge of how to find fish, trusted him to handle boat emergencies. The captain was responsible not only for his boat and crew, but for the amount of fish caught in a season. The captains I knew also felt a sense of responsibility for their crews that extended beyond being at sea together.

In the 1930s significant changes occurred in the fishing industry with the introduction of aerial fish spotting. The factory owners hired airplane spotters to fly along the coast and spot fish. Before aerial spotting, it had been the captain who climbed up in the crow's nest to look for schools of menhaden fish. Sometimes the fish were down so deep under the water that only the eyes of a skilled waterman could see the quick movement or notice the slight change in the surface.

When aerial fish spotting arrived, the captain, confined to the wheelhouse, was forced to wait for information via radio from the airplane spotters. This not only physically changed the role of the captain, but it diminished his position of power.

New technology introduced in the 1950s added aerial fish spotting, that affected the culture of the menhaden industry. Hydraulic hoists were installed aboard the auxiliary boats, more commonly known as *purse boats*. These boats rested in cradles on the deck of the fish boat until put overboard to make "the set" (catch the fish).

The new hydraulic hoists reduced the crew size from fifteen to eight. Prior to this new technology, the chantey man led the crew in singing chants they had memorized while hauling in the heavy nets full of fish. The singing made the men forget being tired. After the introduction of the hydraulic hoists, some older crew members felt their need to sing diminish. Yet these men still had to apply their physical strength while carefully guiding the net so that no fish were lost.

My best friend, Bobbi Gaskins, had a brother, Ryland Gaskins, who became a menhaden boat captain in the early 1960s. After much begging, we convinced him to take us out on his boat. When he finally said yes, we couldn't get our bags packed fast enough.

On Sunday evenings after supper, it was customary for the captain and his mate to check on crewmembers, traveling long dark country roads that took them into small communities where the men and their families lived. If a crewmember needed a ride to the boat, he climbed into the back of the captain's pick-up truck.

On this particular Sunday night, Bobbi and I climbed into the cab of Ryland's truck, ready to head to the factory parking lot, which would already be filled with pick-up trucks and loud machine noises.

We boarded Captain Ry's boat and were sent to the captains' quarters, where we found two bunk beds. I don't recall which one of us got to sleep in the top bunk, as we had been too excited to care about where we slept. We each had a duffle bag filled with clothes that we used as pillows. Once settled in, I lay there in darkness and listened to the sound of the tightened rope that rubbed against the dock piling. The tide had been receding. Before morning, with the bowline untied, the boat gently rocked and bumped against the dock. We left port and headed into the Chesapeake Bay.

When the sun came up, Bobbi and I abandoned our beds and climbed down the outside ladder to the deck below. Unsure about what we should do, we stood at the galley doorway and watched the cook flip pancakes and turn over strips of bacon in a large cast iron frying pan. The noticeable sweat trickled down the back of his neck, disappearing into the collar of his T-shirt. From time to time he lifted his arm, raising it to his brow, and, like a windshield wiper, he swept back the beads of sweat.

In the center of the galley, cheerful men sat on benches at a long wooden table, chatting and chiding one another. The cook, who didn't seem to be paying any attention to the noise, continued refilling empty breakfast platters. And there we were, two teenage girls gazing or probably staring at this crew of black men who looked to be all muscle as they gripped the heavy ceramic coffee mugs with their weathered hands.

They removed their cigarettes, tightly rolled and held in their T-shirt sleeves. It was already hot even though it was early morning. Not a breath of air could be felt. We stood frozen like zombies, until we were noticed, and then the laughter, chiding, and eating ceased. The cook turned and faced us. While still holding his spatula with one hand, he lifted the bottom of his shirt with his other hand and wiped the sweat from his forehead.

"Ladies, have a seat over there at that table. I'll fix you each a nice plate of pancakes, bacon, potatoes, and eggs. Eggs? How many? How would ya like 'um cooked? Boys -- these young ladies are Captain Ry's guests. This one here is his baby sister and her friend. So, I suggest you make them welcome. NOW!"

The men slowly began to rise and leave the galley, but not before saying, "Good morning."

There we sat in silence at the captain's table, in a room that moments earlier had been filled with loud, deep voices. I felt as if I had just crashed a party. But the silence didn't last long. As we ate, the wind picked up and changed our course, encouraging the green flies to enter the galley. The flies began to feast on the dishes of uncovered food before resting on the yellow ceiling above our table. We shooed them away and continued to eat until we heard a voice from the deck above us, followed by the sound of clanging bells.

Curious about the bells, we left the galley, and feeling no relief from the intense heat, we climbed up to the wheel house and looked out, where a man stood at the control panel, lowering the purse boats so that the mate, crew, and Captain Ry could climb aboard. When the two purse boats got underway, Captain Ry with his radio communicated with the airplane spotter overhead. From afar we watched as the mate waved his arms and signaled the crew to let them know the time had come to prepare for a set. The pilot, a ruddy-faced man who grasped the wheel with his stubby fingers as he talked, joined us.

"You girls ever been out on a fish boat before?"

"No sir, Bobbi said. "This is our first trip."

"Well, I tell you, the menhaden are nervous fish. It takes special skills to make sure these fish don't get spooked before we get 'um in the net. Why don't you take Captain Ry's binoculars and watch the set?"

I picked up the heavy binoculars from the edge of the windowsill and zoomed in on the boats that now were far away from us.

※

The only noise in the dead-calm water came from our boat engine and a few hungry sea gulls looking for a handout. The idling engine revved up and we moved forward, headed in the direction of the purse boats. Bobbi and I took turns using the binoculars to watch the boats as they went in opposite directions before dropping the net in the water outside the school of fish.

When the net had been set, the boats completed a circle and then came back together. The school of fish inside the net began to create lots of ripples in the water. I watched the silver streaks move frantically around the top edge of the net. After they discovered they were shut in on one side, the fish bounced on top of the water, still moving rapidly in search of an escape before quieting down. Their glittering scales were now no longer vivid on the surface of the water, and the fish appeared almost lifeless. Gradually fewer fish were near the water's surface, some having already settled on the bottom of the tightly drawn net.

The engine noise had been reduced to a low purring sound. Mesmerized, I watched as the crew dug their fingers into the mesh net, pulling against the weight of the fish. It became difficult to hear above the noise of the hydraulic hoist; yet, an audible chant began, first a single voice, the Chantry man, and then the group response. They sang and guided their net while the strong sunrays beat down on their warm faces, which sparkled with sweat. Short bursts of laughter travelled across the water, announcing a sense of pride. We knew they had won the challenge; the fish had not escaped. Once the net had been lifted, the mate tied the purse boats to our boat, and Captain Ry returned aboard to oversee the bailing operation.

A large tube connected to a pump had been lowered into the net, and it sucked up the small, shiny fish that went into the hold of the boat. The pilot had been right when he said catching fish is an art. But what he forgot to say is keeping the fish is also an art. Over and over that week, the crew exhibited their strength and knowledge of fishing.

We had a good catch that first day, but not good enough to fill up the hold. For several days our boat fished along the coast, making sets each day. Bobbi and I soon tired of watching the process, and we decided to put on our bathing suits. We climbed to the roof of the wheelhouse where we pretended to be sunbathing on a beautiful sand beach. The joy of our fantasy didn't last since we were not allowed to enter the lovely green/blue water.

Overhead an airplane circled. The airplane got so close the pilot's face became visible. Captain Ry talked to the pilot. I didn't know what words were exchanged between the two men, but I heard laughter and the crew teasing their captain about having the best fish bait aboard. Their comments meant nothing, or maybe I just didn't care. After all, we were two teenage girls in search of a good summer tan.

After the fish hold got full, with our boat low in the water, we traveled back to the factory on Friday night. On the approach into the entrance of the creek, gray and pinkish-colored smoke rose from the factory kettle stacks, and the smell of money welcomed us home.

⁓❧⁓

When the fish began to move further north and south, the fish boats traveled beyond the waters of Reedville and Virginia. If the boats needed to off-load fish, they pulled into other factories along the east coast. The boats fished up north as far as New York in the summer and in the fall headed south to Louisiana and Mississippi.

Communications changed because of scanner radios that kept the captains in contact with each other and the airplane pilots, who, unlike the boat crews, could fly home during the week. When the boats were out, the local community knew the status of the week's catch, which boat had made a big haul, and when to expect the boats back in port.

As a result of the modern equipment and work processes, the fishing season expanded into a year-round operation. Some wives followed the boats up north or further south. They caravanned together, drove, talked, and still took care of necessary chores, even hanging wet laundry out of the car windows or across the top of the back seats to dry. But the extended fishing season put more pressure on the wives and children. Families were forced to make hard economic decisions. They had to choose between living here in the Northern Neck and relocating where there were more fish.

The community suffered too. Airplanes collided, and airplane pilots died. Once when a group of wives were travelling south to join their husbands, a terrible automobile accident occurred. A captain's wife and mother of my classmate was killed and others seriously injured. Tragedy had raised its head in our small community where everyone knew everyone or was related. Our community also felt the economic decline after the fishing season expanded away from Reedville. On Saturday nights, cars were no longer parked on Main Street in the local town of Kilmarnock. The stores closed early, and the families of the menhaden fishermen were no longer present to cash paychecks. When Saturday nights in Kilmarnock were absent of people, the town went to sleep.

Years of an ugly legal battle started between commercial (menhaden) and recreational fishermen. The menhaden industry was accused of having over-fished the waters. State and federal agencies got involved. Our local community, determined to fight, demanded better science before more restrictions were placed on menhaden fishing. In late 2012, however, they lost the battle, and more catch limitations were passed against the menhaden industry.

⁓

For more than forty years, the community of Reedville gathers for the Blessing of the Fleet On the first Sunday in May This ancient tradition, held each spring all over the world, celebrates the work of watermen. It is the official opening day of the fishing season on the Chesapeake Bay.

On one occasion I attended this celebration where a crowd of visitors, speakers, and the clergy had gathered. Joined by church choirs, a grand performance occurred, as if it was being televised nationally rather than happening in a small waterfront village in rural Virginia. The audience of locals, week-enders, and retirees like me were present for various reasons. Some had heard family stories about menhaden fishing, others were menhaden fishermen, and then there were those who just wanted to be a part of the celebration. The clergy asked God to bless the fishermen and their boats and to provide a fruitful season.

> *The highlight of the event happened when the parade of boats left from the mouth of Cockrell's Creek and proceeded to the old Morris-Fisher factory, tall-stack property. With assistance from an honor guard from a local American Legion post, a memorial wreath was cast into the water to honor the tradition and heritage of the fishermen who made their living from the water.*

SECTION II:
FROM BARE FEET TO BALL GOWNS

It would be an injustice to this beautiful area I've always called home if I failed to provide insight to the average person's life in and around Kilmarnock during my childhood and teenage years. There were people and places that significantly contributed to my growth. As an adult I longed to come home. I permanently returned in 2003. Home now has a new meaning and offers new experiences.

14 Beauty Queens
15 Saturday Night in Kilmarnock
16 Annual Community Events
17 The Dress
18 Ballroom Dancing
19 Lifetime Friends – A Local Custom
20 Time for a Perm

14

BEAUTY QUEENS

**Photo 25   Gwen Keane, Miss Texaco
Crowned by Dean Loudy**

Television brought the Miss America Pageant into local homes in the 1950s. I watched the yearly event with awe, and yearned to be crowned the queen one day. After years of having May Day queens, local high schools started a homecoming queen tradition. The entire student body voted, and at the half-time celebration during the football homecoming game, a queen and her court were presented to a cheering crowd. The tradition continues today.

As a little girl, I sat by Mama in front of the black-and-white Zenith television set, to watch the annual Miss America beauty pageant, televised each September from Atlantic City, New Jersey. This event triggered my imagination and launched my dream of one day becoming Miss America.

It seemed as if time stood still while waiting for the judges to decide the winner. Long past my bedtime, my head would continue to nod, in spite of my efforts to stay awake.

"Gwen, I think you're sleepy. Do you want me to take you upstairs to bed?"

"No, Mama. I have to see who wins. I like Miss Mississippi. She is so pretty.

Bob Barker, the commentator, slowly opened the sealed envelope received from the judges and announced the third and second runners-up. I remained hopeful that my candidate would win. Finally, he announced the first runner-up, and then he said the magic words, "Miss Mississippi, our new Miss America."

"Oh Mama, she won! I told you so."

Suddenly I became awake and wide-eyed as I watched the winner crowned. Bob Barker burst into song and sang, "Here she comes, Miss America." Tears streamed down her cheeks as she walked the runway and waved to the applauding audience. Upon returning to the stage, the newly crowned queen was joined by her family.

"Oh, Mama isn't she beautiful?"

I continued to ooh and ah while the camera zoomed in on the parents and the younger sister, a homely girl who wore pigtails, braces on her teeth, and horn-rimmed glasses. The sister, so excited, proclaimed that one day she too would wear the crown. The seed had been planted. I then announced my desire to become Miss America.

※

Elizabeth Springer Harrison, a woman of distinction well past the age of sixty, returned home to the Northern Neck in the early 1960s. Her hair, styled and colored blue reminded me of a rock. Nothing could make that hair move. I often wondered how she managed to maintain it. Of course, back then most of us used *Aqua Net* hair spray, the blue plaid bottle that provided extra strong control. I still think *Crazy Glue* was derived from the formula used to create *Aqua Net*.

Mrs. Harrison's beady brown eyes beamed through layers of mascara that coated her long fake eyelashes. Unlike other women in the community, who wore skirts and blouses with peter pan collars and a circle pin, Mrs. Harrison appeared in low-cut dresses that immediately captured the attention and imagination of our local senior-aged men.

Mrs. Harrison, a person with social connections, quickly established herself in the community. Buses loaded with young ladies from the Northern Neck and their evening gowns, accompanied her to Washington, DC, where they attended formal dances, escorted by young cadets from the military service academies.

Mr. Bernstein, a Richmond businessman and personal friend of Mrs. Harrision, brought a LaVogue store to Kilmarnock. Mrs. Harrison who had become active in the promotion of local beauty pageants announced the winner of the Lancaster County Miss Teenage pageant would also be crowned as Miss LaVogue. She would receive a $100 shopping spree at LaVogue, and have the opportunity to compete in Richmond for the title of Miss Teenage Virginia.

Local businesses were contacted and asked to contribute twenty dollars to sponsor a contestant. What a surprise when I answered the telephone and was told "Jackie's Esso Station, Adam's Jewelry Store, and Moore's Florist have sponsored you as a contestant in the upcoming Miss Teenage contest."

My idea of a beauty contest had been to walk out on stage in a beautiful evening gown. But, I soon discovered, hard work lay ahead to prepare for the contest, held at the White Stone Beach pavilion in Lancaster County.

Just like the Miss America pageant, each contestant had to display talent. Rebecca Tebbs, a local college student, volunteered to help the contestants. What could someone like me, who didn't sing or play a musical instrument, do for talent?

Dressed in a Victorian costume that included a wide-brimmed blue straw hat covered in flowers and netting, I danced with a male mannequin and won the 1964 pageant.

The next week the front page of the local Northumberland County newspaper read "Northumberland Girl Chosen Miss Teenage of Lancaster County."

The following year I would be crowned Miss Texaco, queen of the local male softball team.

It had been early fall, and the contestants, dressed in evening gowns, paraded in front of a panel of judges at the season's closing game. The judges selected and announced the names of the three finalists. The winner's name was placed in an envelope and sealed.

Photo 26 The talent contest at the 1964 Miss Teenage contest

Photo 27- Being crowned Miss Texaco

The next spring, the finalist's rode in convertibles in the annual Texaco Parade in Kilmarnock, and with queen-like waves, greeted the crowds of spectators. After the parade, the first ball of the softball season was thrown out to the team in the field. At half time, the finalists walked over to the team manager, Carol Lee Ashburn, and waited for him to open and read the name of the winner. After escorting me to the center of the ball field, I sat in the Holly Ball Queen's gold gilded chair. The Master of Ceremonies, Mr. Dean Loudy, crowned me Miss Texaco. Only two of the three finalists were present for the event. The missing finalist had been pregnant. After the event ended, Mr. Ashburn whispered, "You really were the judge's first choice." We never discussed the subject again.

The following fall, accompanied by Mr. Ashburn and my Grandmother, I went to Richmond as Miss Texaco, where once again I rode in the back of a convertible, waving to the crowds on Board Street, who were there to see the Tobacco Festival Parade.

There were other local beauty pageants held during the 1960's: Miss Flame, Miss Windmill Point, and Miss Rappahannock, to name a few. As times progressed, the local young women became inspired to seek professional careers, and we left the Northern Neck.

The local beauty pageants and the Texaco ball team became things of the past.

15

SATURDAY NIGHT IN KILMARNOCK

Photo 28   Old Fairfax Theater, Main Street
Kilmarnock, Virginia

In the 1950s the menhaden fishing industry was in its prime, and our town, Kilmarnock, awakened on Saturday night. At the factories in Reedville, the week's catch of fish was cooked, and distasteful odors traveled afar, often reaching distant communities like Ditchley, where we lived. I sat on the old porch glider and complained about the awful stink and tried to ignore Grandma's comeback, "Lord, child, that's money you smell

On Saturdays, the fishermen who had been absent all week brought their families to town to cash their payroll checks, shop for groceries, and meet people.

A Saturday night in Kilmarnock was a tradition local families shared. My own family arrived early, hoping to find a good parking spot on Main Street, preferably in front of Norris' Grocery Store.

We rolled down the car windows and waited for people to walk by our car. If it happened to be a neighbor, we exchanged a friendly wave of a hand. But, if someone we rarely saw walked down the street, Grandma poked her head out of the car window and yelled, "Hey, how you been?" This person would leave the sidewalk and join us at the car, leaning against the window while talking.

Alone in the back seat and bored, I escaped by going into Norris' Grocery Store to spend five cents on the purchase of four Mary Jane pieces of candy, plus a piece of bubble gum.

Later, back in the car, while the conversation continued, I happily consumed my Mary Janes, always saving my bubble gum for last. The bubble gum, wrapped in a wax-like paper, was difficult but not impossible to open. Once free of the wrapper, I plunked the hard piece of pink gum into my mouth.

While I chewed, the adults talked. When no one took notice of my presence and the conversation continued, I would use the opportunity to blow bubbles. Sometimes the bubbles popped, and the pink sticky stuff ended up on my face. Determined to rid myself of all evidence before it became time to go home, I used my fingernails to scrape away the mess.

People's Drug Store, located on the corner of Main and Church Streets, was another place where I often retreated. On Saturday night in the drug store, the same group of local businessmen sat at a table sipping cokes and smoking while they discussed the events of the day and shared the local gossip. Once inside the drug store, I would immediately go to the magazine display stand, where I pretended to browse through movie star magazines while listening to the men's conversation and breathing their cigar and cigarette smoke.

The Greyhound Bus that passed through town each day always stopped in front of People's Drug Store. People boarded the bus for the ride to Saluda or Warsaw, where they would transfer and continue their trip further south or north.

The Greyhound bus also transported freight to and from Kilmarnock. Boxes of fresh flowers delivered to the drug store were held until picked up by local florist shop owners.

On Saturday nights, the two Main Street grocery stores, Cockrell's and Norris', were busy places. While the adults shopped, kids went to the Rexall Drug Store located at the corner of Kilmarnock Wharf Road and Main Street.

It was a popular gathering spot for teenagers, offering a full service grill and soda fountain at both the counter and the booths. In a separate area, the teenagers sat in the booths and talked loudly, sometimes throwing food or teasing the waitress. Behaviors changed, though, when Mr. Webb, the owner of the drug store, appeared.

The Fairfax Theater, another popular attraction in the community, was located two doors away from the Rexall Drug Store. The theater had one nightly show Monday through Saturday. Some of the best seats in the house were empty because of the worn seat covers that exposed medal springs.

The faded red velvet curtain, trimmed in gold braid, hung across the stage. While the theater interior could best be described as shabby, the workers made up for the lack of decor.

Thirty minutes prior to show time, Miss Carrie Chase entered the small booth and sold movie tickets. On Saturday nights she also played the theater organ. At the doorway Mr. Brown, the theater manager, locally known as Brownie, collected tickets. Brownie's wife, Miss Mae, poured salt on the freshly made popcorn before scooping it up into the small white paper bags. A bag of popcorn cost ten cents. She also sold the candy, my favorite being a *Sugar Daddy*, because it lasted through the entire movie.

On Saturday nights a drawing would be held. While organ music played, a large wire barrel attached to a wooden frame was brought out from behind the curtain and placed at the center stage. A child from the audience would be chosen to go up on the stage, spin the wheel, and select a winning ticket. I don't remember what was given as the prize. I only recall how much I wanted to be the child that picked the winner. That, of course, never happened!

Two teenager brothers who lived in town routinely created excitement at the Saturday night movie. An unlocked back door allowed one brother to sneak his cocker spaniels into the theater, and during the movie the dogs were let loose to bark, run up and down the aisles, and climb over people's feet. The movie stopped, and through the lobby doors entered Brownie, both arms swinging back and forth while he hurriedly walked down the aisle shouting "Get your dogs and leave here at once."

By the end of the 1970s the Fairfax Theater had closed.

More than fifty years have passed since the economic decline of Kilmarnock, but the memories remain strong of a town that once was energized on Saturday nights.

16

ANNUAL COMMUNITY EVENTS

Photo 29   Ferris Wheel Kilmarnock Fireman's Carnival

People shaped our community. Even today we remain a community of volunteers, the makers and shakers. As time moves on some things go out of fashion; others remain. During 1950-1970, in addition to annual May Days and prom nights, there were other forms of local entertainment.

It occurred once a year in the spring--the annual Minstrel Show produced by the Lion's Club. I now realize this entertainment presented as "fun" was only enjoyable to the white audience. The annual show is as vivid in my mind today as it was more than fifty years ago.

In the old high school auditorium in Kilmarnock, folding chairs were set up. The curtain was pulled open, and on stage sat our well known white professional and business men in the community dressed in striped jackets, bow ties, straw hats with wide colored bands, and blackened faces.

Each participant had a show name. One called himself *Sachamo*. This group of doctors, business owners, the county Commonwealth Attorney, and the district judge told stupid jokes, called each other offensive names, played the banjo and the harmonica, and sang. The chorus included their wives, and sometimes their children participated in a dance. We in the audience laughed until we felt like our ribs ached. Everyone became so overheated from laughter that the paper programs were used as personal fans.

Shamelessly, we applauded and congratulated the cast for their great talent. All of this happened during the era when the *Amos and Andy Show* was broadcast on television.

I do not know when the last minstrel show was presented locally, but I assume when the community became sensitized to the issue of race, it decided to end this annual event. My lifetime friend Bobbi Gaskins and I even copied the idea of blackening our faces when we put together our dance routine for the annual May Day talent contest. We took first place in the school talent show. We never thought about how offensive our act would have been if seen by those in the black community.

This is a childhood memory I am not proud of. However, like so many other things, which happen at different times in our lives, at the time we failed to see the entire picture, and we lacked sensitivity.

⁌⁍

The annual Fireman's Carnival continues to be an event enjoyed by everyone in the community. It has existed for more than seventy years. Back in the 1960s the grand prize on the last night of the carnival was a car. I do not know how or why, but during the summer leading up to the carnival, local teenage girls were allowed to take the car and travel throughout the Northern Neck selling tickets for twenty-five cents each, or five tickets for a dollar. Once when a friend and I took the car out, we ended up in Deltaville at a marina. We were so anxious to sell tickets. I remember we walked down the dock and found some friendly people sitting on their boat. They invited us aboard. As I tried to jump onto the boat, I fell overboard. I was so embarrassed, but we sold a lot of tickets that day.

A unique fact about the Fireman's Carnival is it always opens on the last Thursday night of July, and heavy rains usually occur that week. The carnival runs from Thursday through Saturday, but it never is open on Sunday. After six nights, the carnival is over until the next year. I have heard people say their grandchildren always look forward to attending the carnival. I took our granddaughter to the carnival when she was twelve. I couldn't believe she enjoyed it so much. I commented how I had thought she would be bored since she had been to Disney World several times. Sam responded, "Oh no, this is great. You never have to stand in a line." The carnival is owned, maintained, and operated by our local volunteer fire department.

The firemen and their families work at the carnival. These are folks with full-time day jobs who go out in the middle of the night when called to a fire, and during carnival time they volunteer their time to work there too. My favorite activity at the carnival used to be bingo. But there was no one who loved to play bingo more than Mrs. Mae Munch.

Mae Munch lived across the street from the carnival. I can picture her now walking across the field each night to the carnival and going directly to her favorite corner at the bingo stand. Everyone knew it was Mrs. Munch's corner. Even if someone sat there by mistake, Mrs. Munch in her nasal toned voice would say, "Honey, you got to move over. This is my spot."

And the intruder did move.

During each game, Mrs. Munch played four cards she had personally selected. The winner of the game selected their prize. Oh how I loved the prizes. The selection was better than the offerings at the local Ben Franklin Store on Main Street. The prizes included things like glass candy dishes, tall lamps, or maybe a set of dishes. Just seeing the large variety of prizes made me want to play Bingo.

Today the winners get money. Oh well, who would want a candy dish or a lamp anyway?

The two favorite rides at the carnival were the wooden boats and the metal cars. Everyone standing in line to board the boats raced to get in the boat with the motor. The person in that boat became king-all of the other boats were at the mercy of the king.

Mr. Bob Crowther, owner of the Ford Motor dealership in town, operated the boat stand. He never had a problem getting the youth to assist him. Even the little metal car ride included a favorite vehicle, the fire truck, of course. Clang, clang, clang went the brass bell. Most children who rode that fire truck never stopped ringing the bell until the ride had ended.

───

The old Ferris wheel, even today, continues to attract both kids and adults. There is something special about being up high in the air and being able to see who is at the carnival. "Oh gosh, look over there. So and so is here. Well I'll have to go speak to them when we get off."

We no longer have Saturday night on Main Street in Kilmarnock, but we still have the carnival, a place where people go to meet the people they rarely see. And, of course, the carrousel remains a popular attraction to both young and old. Grandparents stand next to the horse that carries their grandchild up and down on the brass pole. Around and around it goes, as the carnival music travels through the air.

No longer can twenty-five cents buy a ticket for the nightly prize, or for the grand prize- a car. New and more popular stands have been introduced. No, not during my childhood did I get to rock climb, but the younger generations have had that opportunity. And what would the carnival be without their greasy hamburgers, fried onions, and freshly cut French fried potatoes dripping in oil? Thankfully, some things never do change.

17

THE DRESS

**Photo 30   Consignment Shop
Chartes Street, New Orleans, Louisianna**

The store sign on Chartes Street in New Orleans read "Vintage Clothes." In the window a mannequin wore a beautiful lace peach-colored dress. This dress aroused my personal vintage memories of pre-teen years accompanied by my grandmother when I attended the weekly ballroom dance classes. After months of perfecting our dance steps, it was announced we would be having our first semi-formal dance at the country club.

Our small town of Kilmarnock in the early 1960s had two dress stores. The N&P Style Shop was owned by a pleasant *come here*, a Jewish man named Mr. Herbert Pilch. This upscale store carried ladies lingerie, winter coats, furs, dresses, blouses, gloves, hats, and accessories, i.e. costume jewelry. A store with an established reputation, it also sold popular name brand clothes. Just inside the door a sales lady stood, eager to pounce or serve each customer who entered.

There were several sales ladies, and each had different personalities and sales skills. But all of the sales ladies knew everyone in the community and used pleasantries to inquire about the health of family members. Once when I entered the store alone, I was greeted by a demanding voice that asked, "How may I help?"

"Oh, I just want to look around," I responded. Immediately she instructed me to follow her to the back of the store, where the new merchandise was being unpacked. She pushed clothes away that hung on the crowded racks and began removing items. In front of the racks boxes of unopened merchandise blocked the passageway that led to the other side of the store. She showed me coats, pointing out the well-tailored lines and the classic round collars. Fur stoles, jackets, and skins were removed from the racks, and she held them up for me to admire.

"Men shoppers are always in a hurry," she commented, and then she said, "By adding a monogram the gift becomes more personable. Men feel shopping is an unpleasant experience. After all, it's people like me who help make shopping a joyful event." In a stern voice that overshadowed her tightly drawn smile, she told me to return home and tell my grandfather about the selection of beautiful furs available.

Never again did I enter that store alone.

Dunaway's, the other clothing store, was located next door to the N&P Style Shop. They carried clothing and accessories for both women and men. Howard E. Dunaway, the owner of this family-run store, was known locally as a tease, the very opposite persona of his refined wife, Ruth, and his stoic mother, (also named Ruth).

Dunaway's was a spacious store in which garments hung from uncrowded racks. The store presented itself to the customer like a well-set table, inviting, but never overdone.

My grandmother, a frugal person, rarely shopped for store-bought clothes. It never occurred to me that Mrs. Waddy's upcoming semi-formal dance at the country club might justify the purchase of a store-bought dress.

On Fridays, when not in school, my grandmother and I shared a ritual. Seated next to her in a 1955 Chevy station wagon, she drove us to my grandfather's office. Usually I found him standing over his drawing board. Together he and I walked into the other room, where he kept a large black checkbook on the top of his roll top desk. Seated at the desk, he wrote a $25.00 grocery check to Grandma.

On this particular Friday, however, I had not noticed the check was written for $50. Carefully, he recorded the information, then tore the check away from the stub and waved it in the air to dry the ink before he handed it to me.

After arriving in town, the local bank became our first stop. Grandma presented her check and three passbooks to the teller. I want, "five dollars deposited in my husband's Christmas Savings Account, two dollars in mine, and fifty cents in Gwen's."

The teller, nodding her head, date stamped the passbook, and recorded the transactions. The remainder of the check would be carefully spent at our next stop, the grocery store. Once inside the Safeway, with a list in hand, my grandmother selected a few fresh vegetables, fresh fruit, eggs, milk, and a loaf of white bread. Sometimes she added a frying chicken and a piece of beef. Either the chicken or the beef was for Sunday dinner. Depending on the price, a package of pork chops might also be thrown into the cart.

At checkout the total purchases never exceeded fifteen dollars. She stuffed the leftover money into her change purse and later in the week used it to buy more bread and milk. After grocery shopping we returned home - but not on this day. My grandmother drove down Main Street and parked the car right in front of the N&P Style Shop and Dunaways.

First we went into the N&P Style Shop, where I watched Grandma attempt to remove dresses from overcrowded racks. Not finding anything, we went next door to Dunaways. Once inside, Howard E. yelled out his personal welcome. My grandmother had known him and his family all of his life. We walked over to the counter where his wife Mrs. Dunaway stood.

"Do you have any semi-formal dresses that might fit my granddaughter?" Grandma asked.

"I think so," replied Mrs. Dunaway.

From a wall rack she took down several dresses, including a peach-colored lace dress. Having seen my smile, Grandma then reached over and discreetly examined the price tag. "Gwen, "I think you should try on this pretty little dress." Both Mrs. Dunaway and Grandma waited for me until I came out of the dressing room.

Mrs. Dunaway stepped forward and said, "Honey, turn around so I can zip you up."

Then Grandma suggested I raise my arms and turn around slowly.

"You need to make sure this dress is comfortable for dancing."

After she watched me walk around in the dress and flap my arms up and down, like a baby bird trying to fly, she then asked, "What do you think?"

Later at the counter, we stood waiting for my dress, which was being expertly folded, packed with tissue paper, and put into a large cardboard coat box with the name "Dunaways" printed on it.

After Mrs. Dunaway had finished packing the dress, she turned to Grandma and said, "Mrs. Keane, that will be twenty-five dollars."

18

BALLROOM DANCING

Photo 31 The shoe like the one worn by Mrs. Waddy

On hot summer evenings in the southern town of Kilmarnock, Virginia at the Grace Episcopal Church parish house, Mrs. Waddy gave pre-teens ballroom dance classes. The children, like little ducklings, followed her around the room. Sitting in folding metal chairs lined against the wall, mothers watched and fanned themselves with hand-held fans. These were attached to wooden sticks made from cardboard prints of Jesus wearing sandals and a long white robe, his hands outstretched against the background of a glowing light. Above the sound of the dance music, the tall, robust Mrs. Waddy called out, "One, two, three--one, two, three." In Kilmarnock ballroom dancing had arrived.

At the local beauty shops, patrons were given modern-day, puffy, teased, lacquered hair styles. It was the late 1950s, and Mrs. Waddy, a *Come-Here* from New York City, wore her short gray hair in a bob with a side part. It swung across her face like a clock pendulum. Black-netted stockings and short dresses with plunging necklines covered her tanned, leather-like skin.

Mrs. Waddy was different from the locals.

I never knew if there had ever been a Mr. Waddy; however, Herbert, Mrs. Waddy's close male friend, attended each weekly dance class. His job was to manage the record player.

Like most kids, we gossiped and repeated the conversations we had overheard at home. It was after my Grandmother whispered several times, "Poor Mrs. Apple, she doesn't deserve this," I became interested in Mrs. Waddy and her relationship with Herbert.

Herbert routinely staggered into the parish house and collapsed in the corner by the record player. He chain-smoked cigarettes and kept a close eye on Mrs. Waddy. Often, when directed to "stop the music," his attempts resulted in utter failure. Herbert's unsteady fingers reached out to the needle, moving it across the record, creating a horrible scratching sound. I felt embarrassed for him, as he fumbled with the arm of the record player and released several inappropriate words that fell on the ears of the children.

On one occasion after Mrs. Waddy failed to arrive on time, an obnoxious boy in the class self-appointed himself as the "lookout." Ready to announce her arrival, Jimmy peeped through a window blind. He reported when Herbert's truck had pulled up in front of the building.

Herbert, who proceeded slowly, steadied himself by placing his hands on the truck, carefully walking around to the passenger side and opening the door for Mrs. Waddy. Jimmy's laugh called for the rest of us to join him at the window.

Unfortunately for most of us, our window view was blocked, but in almost a whisper, our spy repeated what he saw. Herbert had tried to pull Mrs. Waddy up off the truck seat, but lost his balance. Both he and Mrs. Waddy tumbled into the grass, where she lay on top of him with her dress resting above her waist. According to Jimmy, it was quite a scene, and then he yelled, "Here they come."

We ran back to our seats. Our mothers, who had failed to notice all of the excitement in the room, continued to talk until Herbert and Mrs. Waddy, arm in arm, stumbled into the parish house. Throughout the evening Mrs. Waddy announced several unscheduled breaks, thus enabling her and Herbert to briefly disappear outside. Nothing was ever said about that night, at least not within earshot of us kids.

Mrs. Waddy would reprimand the girls when she noticed poor posture, yet she always ignored the boys, who stood around with stooped shoulders. Don't think the girls didn't notice. When Mrs. Waddy physically corrected a girl's posture, the boys giggled, but those giggles soon turned into "aha," after the girls kicked them in the shins.

Before each new class began she reviewed the previous week's lesson. Mrs. Waddy paired up the couples. For us girls, we either found our hearts beating fast, or we gasped for air when told the name of our assigned partner.

The student who didn't have an assigned partner danced with Mrs. Waddy. I was tall, and when forced to dance with her, my nose rested right between her breasts, which didn't seem to bother her. While we danced she held me close and lifted my feet off the floor as if I were a big sack of potatoes. We circled the room, and I became drunk from inhaling the smell of the lilac toilet water she had splashed on her bosom.

"Now children," she would say. "I must remind you Saturday night is very important. It is our cotillion. Not only is this a formal affair, but it is an occasion when good manners must be exhibited at all times."

I looked over at my friend Bobbi, and we rolled our eyes. We had heard Mrs. Waddy's sermon on etiquette too many times, but this time we got caught, and Mrs. Waddy paired up my friend with the giant boy in our class. Bobbi claimed he always had bad breath, and when he was nervous, which seemed like always, drool escaped from the corners of his mouth.

Because she too was tall, he breathed right in her face as if he was trying to blow a whistle. To make matters worse, he was clumsy and stepped on her feet. I was paired up with the short, fat boy, who used to push his big stomach hard against my body, while squeezing my waist with his hand.

Our summer cotillion was held at the local country club. The girls were dressed in semi-formal dresses and white gloves; the boys wore white dinner jackets. The girls sat on one side of the room, and the boys on the other side. The music began and the boys walked over, bowed in front of a girl, and asked her to dance.

There was also dance competition. We girls stood rigid, wearing a look of distress on our faces as if we were in great pain. The truth was we were too scared to smile for fear of forgetting our dance steps. We just wanted to get through the dance and avoid stepping on our partner's toes or bumping into other couples on the dance floor. Our feet ached in the new shoes, our first introduction to high heels. No, we couldn't take off our shoes and dance in our bare feet. We were never allowed to be barefoot in public.

I guess the weekly Saturday night dances we later attended at the popular White Stone Beach Pavilion were not considered "in public."

At the cotillion, mothers watched with pride, gave nods of approval, and grinned with satisfaction; all secretly hoping their husband's money had been well spent on the dance classes. After all, their children were now prepared for bigger and better things in life, like future high school proms and the annual debutante Holly Ball.

Photo 32 Emily Keane on her 90th birthday
Playing the harmonica

19

Lifetime Friends
A Local Custom

While growing up here in the 1950s, watching television was not the acceptable pastime that it is today. In winter, Grandma kept her rocking chair in the archway between the dining room and the living room. When summer arrived, the rocking chair was moved to the screened-in porch. On most nights, I sat on Grandma's lap with my head snuggled against her breasts, I asked her to tell me a story.

Grandma usually reminisced about having been raised on the plantation *Bushfield* in Westmoreland County. She had been one of seven Detrick children. During her childhood in the early 1900s, guests traveled long distances, either by horse and buggy or boat, to visit friends or relatives. Most of the guests stayed at least two weeks. Thus, Grandma had developed a close friendship with one of the Kelly girls, Gertrude, who lived in Balls Neck in Northumberland, an entire county away.

After Gertrude married Walter Harvey, they lived in *Cobbs Hall*, the family home. In the late 1930s after Grandma and Granddaddy had married, they returned to his family home in Ditchley. The two childhood girlfriends, Emily and Gertrude, were now neighbors living three miles apart and raising their own families.

Communications had improved because of bicycles and cars. Telephones were not available to everyone. In most communities neighbors shared a single telephone line. The years passed as Grandma's and Gertrude's friendship continued to grow and strengthen.

When I was a young adult, I remember Gertrude, who was almost blind telling me how Grandma had become her eyes, and she was Grandma's knees. Each week Grandma drove to *Cobbs Hall* and picked up Gertrude, taking her to Kilmarnock to grocery shop. After parking the car, with arms locked together, they walked to *Lee's Restaurant* and had lunch.

Grandma would read the menu to Gertrude. When it was time to leave, Gertrude stood up and offered her shoulder to Grandma for support. With Grandma leading the way, they returned home.

It was a cold winter evening and I was living in Washington, D.C. That night I called Grandma, who then was in her late 80's, and asked her how the day had been. She said, "I visited Gertrude today. After tea we decided that in spite of the cold weather, it was a good day to wade out into the water and pick up some oysters to have for supper."

Grandma had shucked the oysters for her and Gertrude to share. Hours later, here she was still pleased with the day's catch, although she had been so chilled she put on her socks and crawled into bed early. My phone call had interrupted her listening to a nighttime radio talk show. Years later I learned that she enjoyed listening to the Dr. Ruth show and had been entertained by the callers seeking advice on sex.

As these two lifetime friends continued to age, going out together became less frequent, but they talked by phone every day. It was sad when Gertrude died. She left behind her devoted friend Emily Keane, who never recovered from the loss.

Concerned that Grandma spent too much time alone, I suggested she make some new friends, as new people had moved into the community. Repeatedly I made this suggestion.

Finally, Grandma said, "These new people show up from somewhere. They can say anything they want, but that doesn't mean it's the truth. They could be murderers for all I know."

Grandma died believing lifetime friends are the only real friends a person can have. Grandma was a good representative of Local Color, bless her heart

20

TIME FOR A PERM

Photo 33   The Toni Permanent

When I was a little girl and there was an upcoming event such as taking school pictures or getting ready for my first formal dance, my grandmother would call Little Ruth and set up an appointment for me to get a Toni permanent wave.

Miss Ruth operated a beauty shop in her home. There was no special equipment. Everything took place in her kitchen. First I'd bend my head over her kitchen sink while she stood on a stool and washed my hair. Afterwards I sat at her kitchen table awaiting the dreaded process. Miss Ruth would suddenly stop talking and pick up the rat end of her comb she used to part my hair into sections, holding them in place with large aluminum hair clips. A few ends of my hair were then placed in small folded sheets of tissue paper and rolled into a curler. There were pink, white, and purple curlers. Miss Ruth said each color meant they were different sizes, and she had to use the small pink curlers for the top of my head to make sure I got a puffy hairstyle. To me, all of the curlers looked the same.

After all of the curlers had been used, Miss Ruth would take absorbent cotton and make a band to wrap around my head before she applied the bottle of setting solution. I was then handed a towel to hold, just in case the stuff ran down my face. And I remember how she always double-checked to make sure the entire contents of the bottle had been used. Grateful for the towel, I sat there blotting away the clear liquid as it ran down my cheeks. Once Miss Ruth was satisfied each curler had been appropriately soaked with the solution, she set the kitchen timer.

When the timer rang, I'd return to the kitchen sink to have my head covered in curlers rinsed in hot water before Miss Ruth applied the neutralizer. Oh, did I hate that stuff. It smelled like ammonia. I would cough, and she'd give me a glass of water.

She removed the cotton wrap and placed a plastic cap over my head before leaving the room to retrieve the portable hair dryer stored in a small vinyl suit case. At one end of the machine was hose like that used on canister vacuum cleaners. The plastic hood attached to the other end of the hose, which she carefully placed over my head, making sure not to disturb the rollers.

When the button was turned to the On position, the hood filled up with air, and there I sat for 15 minutes. Afterwards, I returned to the kitchen sink, where Miss Ruth carefully unwound each curler after she had checked to make sure the permanent had taken. Convinced I had plenty of curls, she then would spray my head with more hot water, before removing the plastic curlers.

Sometimes when it had been quiet for a long time, Miss Ruth talked about something she had recently heard or read. She wasn't a gossiper. She liked new beauty tips. Once she said that during my next visit, she would use a *Lilt* home permanent. She had seen an ad in a movie magazine. I told her it would be good if it smelled better than that *Toni,* but later I discovered it didn't and learned that some things just never change

After again sitting down at the kitchen table, I would wait for Miss Ruth to return with the plastic box of pink wire brush rollers. These rollers, like the plastic curlers, covered my head and were held in place with little sharp pieces of plastic that looked like tiny swords.

Occasionally Miss Ruth would reach over and turn off the dryer so that she could check my hair. When she was convinced my hair was dry, she took off the hood and removed the wire brush rollers, even those that didn't want to be released from my hair.

I knew better than to complain when the skin on my scalp was being pulled, because Grandma would have been unhappy to hear I had misbehaved. Miss Ruth, who held a big bristled brush in her hand, pulled hard to get it through my thick hair. Then, using her small delicate fingers, she separated each curl and patted it softly with the palms of her hands. When she was finished, *Aqua Velvet* hair spray was applied. It held every hair in place until the next washing.

Miss Ruth, who was a nice lady, would then give me a bacon, lettuce, and tomato sandwich and a glass of sweetened iced tea. I was never happy, though, to go to her house for a perm because it took most of a day--not to mention that horrible smell. I thought skunks smelled better than my hair.

Miss Ruth had two children, a girl and a boy. The girl was in my grade at school, but most of the time she lived with her grandparents. Her father was an only child, so the grandmother enjoyed having a little girl around that she could dress up. The boy was a couple of years younger. I didn't know him well, but I remember him being very skinny and not looking healthy.

In the late 1970s when I had come home one weekend to see my Grandmother, I took her to Lee's Restaurant on Saturday for lunch. While sitting in a booth I noticed two people who looked familiar to me sitting at a table near the front of the restaurant. A third menu was placed at their table.

I commented to Grandma that I was sure Little Ruth's mother-in-law and daughter had arrived. Grandma said we must stop by their table when we were ready to leave.

I watched the front door open and a very skinny woman with long blonde hair appeared. She wore a red dress, stockings, and red high heels, and she carried a red purse. Her walk was unsteady as she headed towards the table at the front of the restaurant. Clearly she was not used to walking in the high heels.

Her face looked familiar, but I wasn't sure who she was. When we got ready to leave and stopped at the table to speak to Little Ruth's mother-in-law, she introduced us to her two granddaughters. Once we were out on the street Grandma said, "I thought she only had one granddaughter and one grandson."

> *"Yes Grandma, you are correct," I replied. Before the day had ended gossip was all over town that the grandson had undergone a sex change. For many months that was the big topic of conversation in our little town of Kilmarnock.*

SECTION III –
PLACES AND PEOPLE MAKE THE COMMUNITY

Every town has its characters who define how people feel about their hometown. There are the strong-minded ladies and the local businessmen. Then there are those who make the town "bloom." As a child, if I didn't personally know these people, my family did. Therefore, in my mind, all of them represent local color. Some behaved in a manner I didn't understand. Others expressed themselves in a way that added entertainment to the conversation at the supper table. Then there were the givers in the community, those who helped make our town a better place to live and visit. In this section, I reveal people and events that formed my attachment to Kilmarnock and my willingness to call it my hometown, although I lived in the community of Ditchley, four miles away.

21 Mama No and Daddy Wil
22 Cousin Pearl
23 The Eubank Family
24 The Adams Brides
25 Miss Enid and Family
26 Lou Baker
27 Claudine Curry Smith
28 Born Into the Funeral Business
29 Ditchley Landscape
30 Some More Equal than Others

21

MAMA NO AND DADDY WIL

Photo 34   Nora and Willie George

In-laws fall into one of two categories--you take 'um or leave 'um. My in-laws, Nora and Willie George, Lancaster County natives, were definitely in the take 'um category. To family they were just "Mama No and Daddy Wil," typical people of their era, who raised three children during the depression and post-war years. I chose to write about them, because to me they are perfect examples of local hard-working people who shared their life with family, neighbors, and church. I hate to think what they would say today if they could watch reality television shows. And I can't imagine how Nora would have adapted to "just in time" microwave cooking.

Foxwells, Virginia, where Nora and Willie lived, is a community that still exists today. All who lived in Palmer, Foxwells, or Goat Island (later renamed Westland and now called Windmill Point) were known as "island people." These were people who made their living as watermen.

Nora, tall and slender, wore her black, wavy hair in a French twist. Each morning after breakfast, she put on her makeup and got dressed. Even if she was going to clean her house, she wore a nice dress, seamed stockings, high heels, and an apron. She was a stay-at-home wife and mother who took care of family finances and anything else related to home. The finances were simple. The family saved their money and paid cash for everything.

I was a teenager when I first met my future in-laws. Willie, a short, stocky man with stubby fingers and wide hands, had reddish-colored skin earned from years of working as a waterman. Although he never complained, he did comment about the dark mornings when he got up at 3:00 a.m. to go out on Captain Odell Fitchetts' boat.

The boat was kept in Palmer, a five-minute ride from Foxwells. It was important to get out into the bay and fishing by sun-up. Joe, one of the crewmembers, worked as both a "hand" and a "cook." Willie, who remembered his mother's good cooking, often spoke of how many biscuits he had eaten each morning aboard the boat.

When Willie wasn't fishing, he mended net with his brother Reuben and another man. They worked in a field next to an open fire contained in a barrel. Net menders passed their skills on to the next generation. A net needle and twine were used to mend holes before the net was dipped into a barrel of hot tar to seal the repairs. I was fascinated by the men's skills. Sometimes if I saw the men working in the field, I stopped and watched them mend nets. I remember the smell of the tar that never disappeared from their work clothes and their hands of rough, worn skin covered in calluses. Not once did anyone complain about the work being too hard. It put food on the table. It was a requirement for survival. These net menders worked long hours before they ever took a cigarette or a lunch break. Their lunch of leftover supper was carried in a black, metal-hinged lunchbox. In the top of the box a wire cradle held a thermos of hot coffee.

⊙≫

At the end of the day, Willie, who rode with Captain Fitchett, stopped at Beagle's store in Foxwells. This was the local social hub for the workingman. In the winter months, the watermen came in around 4 p.m. to warm up by the stove, buy a soda or cigarettes. Behind the cash register Margie Sommers rang up the purchased items. Margie, a maiden lady, didn't say a lot. She just stuck to her job. But the men always had something to say. They exchanged news and gossip and teased each other.

Every afternoon when Willie got to Beagle's store, he called Nora to ask if there was anything he should pick up for supper. On one occasion Nora requested a box of napkins. Willie failed to clean his fogged-up eyeglasses before he grabbed a box of napkins from the bottom shelf. When he got home, he set the table and opened the new box of napkins, only to discover he had purchased women's sanitary napkins.

An embarrassed Nora called Beagles store and told Margie what had happened. Margie's response was "Yes, Miss Nora, I know."

For a long time Willie's mistake was the topic of light conversation at the Sunday dinner table. A good-natured Willie laughed at himself. But we always wondered what Margie had thought when she checked Willie out that evening. Margie never missed anything, including the opportunity many years later to become the second Mrs. Beagle. Margie continued to work for her husband until he retired and closed the store.

Like many men of his generation, Willie had stories to tell, his favorite being about his American Indian heritage. He told of how his grandfather had married an Indian squaw. At that time, interracial marriages were against the law in Virginia. Therefore, his grandmother had lived in the marsh.

Willie was a private person who never talked about himself. Nora said before Willie lost his money in the depression, he had been a different man, a proud independent fisherman. And it was a sad day when he borrowed money from the bank to pay his crew to pull his nets and put his boat ashore.

Willie never talked about that part of his life. Nora said the experience had made him nervous. After that tragedy, Nora took over all of the family finances.

During Nora and Willie's early years of marriage they lived with Willie's parents. They had their first two children living there also. Nora, tired of living with the in-laws, decided she would save enough money to build their own house. In 1943, Nora and Willie rode with their builder to Tappahannock, where Nora hand-selected lumber for their new home, ensuring each board was free of knots and warp. Nora, proud of their home, always said she had shortened her kitchen, because during the war building materials were scarce. Before they moved, Nora gave birth to their third child, a son.

Neither Nora nor Willie had a driver's license. On Saturday morning, Nora sat at the telephone table with her handwritten grocery list and called in her grocery order to Beagle's Store. Her order always included five hand-dipped scoops of vanilla ice cream and five scoops of chocolate. By two o'clock Mr. Beagle arrived at Nora's back door and unloaded her groceries. No money was ever exchanged until the end of the week when Nora sent Willie to pay Mr. Beagle.

Nora cooked on Saturday afternoons. Before the roast beef was put in the oven, she made a yellow layer cake from scratch and smothered it in a dark chocolate boiled icing. Nora then cooked a piece of ham or a roast and made her famous home-cooked potato salad dressing. She wasn't finished until she had cooked potatoes, macaroni and cheese, deviled eggs, and collard greens. On Sunday morning before she left for church, Nora fried the small chicken breasts that had soaked in salt water overnight. Before her Sunday guests arrived she mashed the potatoes and made gravy.

Sunday at noon all of Nora's hard work was put on display in the dining room. The family arrived, entering through the back door. Nora stood in the kitchen ready to receive hugs and comments about the good smells that filled the house. After everyone was seated, Edward J., the son-in-law, spoke. "Mama

No sure can lay out a good spread." A blushing Nora then would ask Edward J. to say the grace. At the end of the meal, although everyone felt like a stuffed turkey, no one ever refused dessert. When the homemade cake was served, guests were offered a scoop of vanilla or chocolate ice cream.

For most of the week, the supper menu was chosen from the food Nora had cooked over the weekend.

Nora also took care of her mother, Mrs. Raines. They both enjoyed weekly visits from one or more preachers. Each time a preacher visited, he walked into a clean house, received a warm welcome, and was offered a slice of Nora's cake.

The Foxwells community had both a Baptist and a Methodist church. For many years, Willie, a Baptist, and Nora, a Methodist, attended both churches on Sunday with their children. The Baptists held morning services and the Methodists had an afternoon service. In later years after two of their children were grown, both churches held Sunday morning services only. Willie remained a faithful Baptist, taking his son to church with him, while Nora, a devoted Methodist, attended her church every Sunday.

Willie lived well into his nineties and Nora lived beyond the age of a hundred. When Nora died, she was the last living child of a Confederate soldier in the state of Virginia.

22

COUSIN PEARL

Photo 35　Moon shining through the trees in Ditchley

Every family has secrets. Like a ball of string thrown on the floor, the truth unravels, and soon we discover the unknown relatives. New stories emerge, and now someone like Cousin Pearl is no longer a stranger but is family.

I did not know where we might be going after we left home that Sunday afternoon. My grandfather said it would be difficult to find the old home place. We parked the car on the side of the road, climbed over the wire fence, and walked fast through the animal-inhabited property, where cows grazed.

The old, dilapidated house, wrapped in vines and covered with undergrowth, became visible as we exited the dense woods. This peninsula of land, right off of Remo Road, faced a creek not far from the Chesapeake Bay. A single oak tree stood tall between the house and the bank, with big shapely branches that stretched in every direction. On top of the hard soil, enormous tree roots rested.

I looked up at the old oak tree and tried to imagine how someone might have once sat in a swing attached to the lower limb or might have just used it as a place to rest. I wondered what Cousin Pearl could have done here when she had been a little girl?

My grandparents and I entered the abandoned house and found ourselves standing in the entry hallway amongst broken objects and scattered papers on the floor. The house had been vandalized over the years. I couldn't imagine how anyone could have found this house unless by boat. Granddaddy said the house had been vacant for thirty years. And on this particular Sunday, instead of going for a drive, my grandparents and I had gone to find the old home place, deserted by Pearl Lee Boone.

A doctor from St. Elizabeth's Hospital in Washington, D.C. had called on Saturday and announced the death of

Cousin Pearl, a name that meant nothing to me, an eleven-year-old, but I did want to know more about this unknown cousin. My grandparents explained the blood relationship, but I still didn't understand why we had to find the family home. Under the stairs in the entry hall, I found an open door and peeped inside the small closet. Across the back wall there remained a row of rusty nails. Each nail held a different pattern of knotted string.

"Granddaddy, what is this?" I asked.

"Pearl's hex signs. After she threatened to put a curse on someone, she made a hex sign out of string."

I had more questions but decided to wait.

I entered the dining room followed by my grandparents. Furniture filled the room, but the rain that had entered through the leaky roof had not ruined it. Pieces of broken china covered the floor. The side tables were topless. Grandma said the marble tops had been stolen.

I became interested in the round pedestal walnut table and the chairs decorated in hand-carved butterflies. The rotted upholstery revealed the existence of the original seaweed stuffing.

Granddaddy, who had walked over to a chair, reached out with his wrinkled hand and gently touched the chair back.

"Your great-great-grandfather made this table and chairs. I knew the dining room set had gone to Aunt Molly when the siblings divided up the family furniture. I just never thought I'd see it again."

"Who is Aunt Molly?" I asked.

"She is Pearl's mother. Molly Lang."

I felt an urge to ask more questions but chose not to since I still had so much to see.

⁓⃟

The bright sunlight poured through what once had been a window and cast shadows on the wooden floor. I noticed a small object that appeared to be a skeleton wrapped around the base of the pedestal table. Grandma asked, "Carter, can that be the little dog Pearl used to have?

"Yep. That's what it looks like. Pearl probably just drove back to Bladensburg and forgot to take it with her. "

I did not want to hear any more of this conversation, so I left the room. In the entry hallway I found the stairs and climbed to the top, where I stood amongst old papers and checks that littered the entire floor. I picked up a check. It had been issued by a New York City bank, and had been written to Molly Lang. All of the letters on the floor were from Pearl. Whoever the intruders had been, they stole more than physical objects. Pieces of Cousin Pearl's life lay open to be examined by strangers.

When Granddaddy reached the top step, I handed him some of the checks. In return, he gave me a paper bag and said I should gather up the checks so he could contact the bank and find out if Cousin Pearl ever closed the account. Not only did I pick up all of the checks, but I also gathered the letters. I wished to protect this unknown cousin. Why should strangers be allowed to read the letters written by a devoted daughter?

I returned back downstairs and entered the living room, where I found unopened crates of books. 1 grabbed at the wooden slats that imprisoned the books with my fingers. After releasing the books from the crate, I discovered three different volumes, all hard bound in a rich green-colored backing. Each contained sketches of crabs and other marine life. Printed on the front of the books in gold lettering were the words "Vanderbilt Marine Museum." I began to think these books might be important, and then I saw her name, Lee Boone. Cousin Pearl had been the author.

Grandma and Granddaddy were no longer in the house, and there all alone, I found myself with crates of books and the bones of Cousin Pearl's little dog. I gathered up copies of the books and hurried outside to find my grandparents. Under the big oak tree beside a large ribbed aluminum structure stood my grandparents. The structure looked like a big doghouse. When I asked, "What is this thing?" Granddaddy said, "It is a cover over Mrs. Lang's grave." There had been no tombstone, and this object didn't look like anything I had ever seen in a graveyard.

Granddaddy spoke of how Cousin Pearl had slept on her mother's grave for weeks and then decided to go back to Bladensburg, Maryland. Before leaving she had the thing built and put over her mother's grave.

"What happened to Cousin Pearl?" I asked. My eyes followed as my grandfather turned and faced Grandma before he bent over and picked up a small stick.

Then, as if showing frustration, he threw the stick back onto the ground. I waited and watched. Why wouldn't he just tell me what had happened?

Finally, while staring down at the grave, Granddaddy told his story. He had learned 20 years earlier Pearl's house in Maryland had been condemned to make way for a new highway. She refused to leave the house even after the electricity and water had been cut off. A judge then decided she couldn't take care of herself and had her admitted to St. Elizabeth's, a psychiatric hospital. Without any more information, Granddaddy stopped talking, raised his hand, and motioned for us to leave. The three of us walked in silence back to the car, me carrying the letters, checks, and books I had collected.

Once inside the car, eager to know more, I began to ask questions. We had left Wicomico Church and were driving on Route 200 headed towards Ditchley. Grandma, who tried to change the subject and not talk about Cousin Pearl, commented on the yard decorations we passed and the cute little wooden cart filled with flowers in someone's yard.

A few miles further down the road, she and Granddaddy finally gave up trying to distract me and began to reminisce about this unknown family member.

Granddaddy said when he had been the Manager of the East Coast Utility Company Pearl came to Kilmarnock one morning and parked her old car in front of his office. When she came in the door, he heard her cursing. But worst of all, she had been dressed in a flannel nightgown. Granddaddy, being a gentleman, walked her back to the car and discovered no front seat. Cousin Pearl had been sitting on a stack of old tires.

I asked if Pearl had lived with her mother. Since I didn't live with my mother, this interested me. Granddaddy said she had been an only child and her mother's whole world. She left her mother to attend college, and Mrs. Lang never forgave her.

Now intrigued with this newly found relative, I began to read aloud the contents of the letters I had just acquired.

"Listen" I said.

"Teddy and I are so enjoying our winter in Florida. He brings the wheelbarrow down to the garden and helps me load it up with the fresh vegetables we have grown."

I stopped reading and ask, "Who is Teddy?"

My grandparents wanted to avoid answering my question and tried to steer the conversation to the type of individual Cousin Pearl had been. Granddaddy began by saying, "Pearl never had an ounce of common sense, but other people, well-respected professional people, described her as being brilliant. She had been a marine biologist who worked for the Smithsonian Museum in D.C. Sometime later she had been hired by the Vanderbilt Marine Museum. She worked for Mr. William K. Vanderbilt II, a ship owner, who came from the wealthy Vanderbilt family in New York. They travelled together, and she wrote books about their explorations."

Back at home, I emptied the bag of Cousin Pearl's handwritten letters. In her letters, she gave details of her day. She would begin with a description of the sunrise and end by describing the sunset. Most of her letters mentioned Mr. Vanderbilt. Whether the letters described a fantasy or reality, even at age eleven, I became suspicious that Cousin Pearl and Mr. Vanderbilt had been romantically involved.

Grandma told my daddy about Pearl's old home place and what we had found during our visit. A few days later, early in the morning, I saw Daddy's skiff coming into the creek with something piled high near the bow. I greeted him at the dock and immediately recognized the furniture.

"Daddy, did you get those chairs from Cousin Pearl's place?" I asked.

Daddy said nothing and began walking towards the house. In the kitchen, we sat at the table with Grandma. Daddy, who we always said "is not afraid of the devil," began recounting his experience of the night before when he had visited Cousin Pearl's property.

He began his story by explaining he decided to go there because it had been a full moon.

"Are you crazy? Why would you go all the way up there in that little boat of yours?" Grandma muttered.

"For God's sake, Mama, let me tell my story. When I got there, I pulled my boat up on shore, climbed the bank, and went inside the house. I just wanted to get a couple of chairs that my great-grandfather had made. I figured everyone else had been in the house and stolen things, so why shouldn't I get a few chairs? "

"Sonny, I can't believe you did this. You had no right to those chairs."

"Well, right or not, I got the chairs. First, I picked up a side chair. It was heavy. I knew I'd have to make several trips. I managed to load it on the boat. Then I went back and got a second side chair and loaded it on the boat. On the third trip, I had an armchair, and just as I got to that big old oak tree where the limb swings down in front of Aunt Molly's grave, I stopped to rest."

"Sonny, I think I would have rested someplace else other than in front of Mrs. Lang's grave."

Now I had become the one who wanted Grandma to stop talking so I could hear the rest of daddy's story.

"Mama, are you going to let me finish?"

"Okay. Tell your story."

"Well, I then heard laughter, and when I looked up at that tree, there sat Pearl. I saw Pearl, and she had on a long nightgown. She laughed at me. I picked up that armchair and ran down the bank. I threw it in the boat, and started home."

"Sonny, you are making that up. You didn't see Pearl on that limb, and dead people don't laugh."

"No Mama, you are wrong. I saw Pearl, and I'll tell you something else. As much as I want the rest of those dining room chairs, I am never going back to that place. Pearl had been crazy when alive, and she's still crazy dead."

23

THE EUBANK FAMILY

**Photo 36 The Turner House on Church Street, Kilmarnock, Virginia
It was originally the Eubank House
Now the Kilmarnock Inn**

For more than 115 years, the Eubank Family owned and operated its business in Kilmarnock. The family is remembered for its generosity to those in the community.

On May 1, 1886 Silas William Eubank, father of Enid Edmonds Eubank and his brother Warner Augustus Eubank, established the Eubank and Brother Store.

This store provided local residents with food, farming implements, and general merchandise (including a designated millinery section). This store served as the community bank, in which the brothers became business advisers. Their reputation for honesty and fair dealing was so firm that their due bills "Pay to bearer $___ in merchandise" became the local currency. The store, known throughout the county as a general gathering place, was also where regular customers could get extended credit.

In addition to the store, the Eubank brothers built and operated a hotel as well as a restaurant and livery stable, much used by drummers (traveling salesman of old).

In 1901 they bought the 338-acre Waverly Avenue Farm and constructed a steamboat wharf, used as a regular point of landing. They developed the Wharf Road (Augustus Avenue) in 1902 and also established the Eubank Tankard Company, a menhaden fish factory.

The frame-structured Eubank and Brother Store was destroyed by fire on November 13, 1909. In 1910 the Eubanks rebuilt on this same site, and constructed the two-story brick building that still exists today on Main Street, one half occupied by Peoples Drug, which is now where the Anchor Pharmacy resides. The Eubank and Brother Store remained in business for more than fifty years, the brothers never retiring, continuing to attend to the store as their health permitted.

In 1947 Joseph H. Adams and his wife Laura Anna Turner Adams, the granddaughter of Silas William Eubank, established the Adams's Jewelry Store on Main Street in Kilmarnock (in a portion of the building known as Nobletts today).

In 1958, after another fire severely damaged the building of the former Eubank and Brother Store the building was renovated, and the Adams' Jewelry store relocated to that building. The Adams owned and operated their store for more than sixty years. Today the ladies' dress store Foxy resides in the part of the building formerly known as Adams Jewelry.

This little bit of history sets the scene for what follows--

Photo 37   Joe Adams and Laura Anna Turner Adams
The first summer after their wedding
Jamestown, Virginia

24

THE ADAMS BRIDES

For more than sixty years, Mr. Joseph H. Adams and his wife Laura Anna owned and operated their jewelry store on Main Street in Kilmarnock. When I was a teenager in high school, I worked part-time at a local florist shop. I had the opportunity one day to wait on Laura Anna Adams. That night she called me at home and asked if I would be interested in working at her store. Little did I know then how much influence she would have on my life, and how she would remain in my heart forever. Laura Anna Turner Adams died March 9, 2001.

With Christmas two days away, the heavy snowfall would provide us with a white Christmas and a shortened holiday shopping season. Rather than stay in the store and wrap Christmas gifts, I chose to ride with Mr. Adams, transporting beautifully wrapped bridal presents.

The falling snowflakes disappeared quickly on the windshield of Mr. Adam's new Ford station wagon. Determined, he carefully drove across the Wicomico River Bridge, while I sat in silence and relived memories of the previous summer. I had met many brides to be, including Mary Jane.

I remembered there hadn't been any customers that morning, but I had kept busy wrapping graduation and wedding presents. When I heard the sound of the bells on the door jingle, I moved to the front of the store to greet the customer, except there were two. The older woman, beautifully dressed in a navy blue suit and a straw hat with a spray of flowers, carried a linen cloth handbag that matched her high heels. I never noticed what the young woman was wearing because my eyes gravitated to the unmanageable hair that engulfed her face like a wind-blown veil.

When I asked how I could help them, the older woman spoke. She let me know she was the mother of the young woman with her, Mary Jane. They had an appointment with Mrs. Adams. The mother was quick to say her daughter wanted to select china and crystal patterns only, since she already had inherited silver flatware from her maternal grandmother.

The mother, who I thought was trying to intimidate me, curtly asked if I was familiar with the Gorham silver pattern *Steiff Rose*.

When I said "yes," she raised her eyebrows and turned to her daughter.

Then I thought she was trying to win me over when she commented something about "...Mrs. Adams always hires bright young ladies". She also told me she too had once been an Adams bride and that now it was her daughter's turn, because she would be married December 24th.

I knew I didn't like this woman, but after all she was a customer. Then she tried to impress me when she said the groom to be was a wonderful local young man from a very connected family--the Lee's and the Carters. I almost burst out laughing, but it got worse. She added that her family also was a direct decedent of William Carter. It's hard to forget people like that, a mother who held herself in high esteem based on her ancestry. I guess my accent gave me away, because she let me know I too must be local. Thankfully Mrs. Adams then entered the store.

People who knew Laura Anna always made comments about her erect posture and her expensive clothes. On this day she wore a linen Villager suit with pearls and other fine gold jewelry. Laura Anna, late as always, hastened past me and the customers. She walked straight over to her desk, where she emptied an armload of paperwork and her purse, all the while chatting and apologizing for being late.

Continuing to talk, Mrs. Adams tactfully guided the conversation to the topic of weddings, as she moved across the room and joined the mother-daughter duo. I watched them from the other side of the room. Standing erect behind a display counter, she picked up a light green table mat that would be used to demonstrate table settings. Carefully she proceeded to select china plate samples from the wall display and placed them on the mat one at a time. I was so intrigued with what was happening, I stopped wrapping presents so that I could watch and listen to the conversation.

Mrs. Adams first presented a traditional china pattern, which was plain but elegant.

The mother reacted with harsh antics as if she were going to faint and moaned, "Oh, no." She didn't think it suited her daughter and told Mrs. Adams they had something a little more elaborate in mind.

But Mrs. Adams, being a pro, knew exactly how to handle the mother. She chose a plate with a band of dark green and gold scroll trim. She indicated that the pattern was very elaborate, and it was fine bone china.

Before the mother could say anything, Mrs. Adams placed a piece of crystal stemware next to the plate. She knew her customers and could see that this woman would keep her busy all day, unless she took control of the situation.

I couldn't stop watching the dynamics between these two, while the daughter said nothing.

Then Mrs. Adams suggested the plate she had put on the mat might be too formal, as she turned and touched another plate on the wall display. This plate was covered in violets. Mrs. Adams told the duo that violets were very in this year. The mother stepped back and turned her head. She told Mrs. Adams a plate decorated with violets was definitely inappropriate for her daughter. Mrs. Adams had tricked the mother, and she had won.

Suddenly the mother favored the plate with the green and gold band. She even described how beautiful it would look on Mary Jane's Thanksgiving table, and that it would go well with the grandmother's silver flatware pattern.

Mary Jane still did not speak but gave a nod of approval.

Changing the subject, the mother then asked what was the crystal pattern next to the plate. Mrs. Adams told her it was a pattern by Gorham, called *Dolly Madison*.

The mother waved her hand in the air and gave a smile of approval.

Mary Jane, like a trained dog, again nodded her head.

By four o'clock the mother-daughter duo had agreed on patterns and signed the bridal registry. All afternoon Mary Jane had non-verbally approved her mother's recommendations. The bride-to-be selected two china patterns, one of fine bone china for special occasions, and another for everyday use. She selected a cut glass crystal stemware pattern (requesting eights in sherbets, iced teas, and goblets) that would be used with her fine bone china. For everyday use, she chose a heavily weighted gold color crystal stemware from Fostoria called *Jamestown*. Although Mary Jane already had eight place settings of her grandmother's silver pattern, she said she would be happy to receive extra serving pieces. Well, that was the moment of surprise! Until then I assumed Mary Jane had a speech problem, like a lisp, but in reality her only problem was a domineering mother.

All summer and fall, the duo frequently visited the store, or sometimes it would just be the mother and a friend who came in and asked to be shown Mary Jane's patterns. By October Mary Jane's name had been inscribed on a place card and her pattern selections were set on a table with a lace cloth next to the front door. In addition to the display of her silver, china, and crystal, there were sterling silver candle sticks that held white candles and a small centerpiece of plastic flowers to accent the eloquent place setting. Mary Jane's informal china and crystal selections were set up on the bottom shelf of a display case. Now everyone could see what the bride-to-be had chosen and could discreetly inquire about prices. Some customers were interested in finding an appropriate shower gift, while others selecting a wedding present placed a special order for a serving piece in her silver or china patterns. During visits from the mother, the bride-to-be, and their friends, without asking we soon learned complete details of the wedding, the wedding gown, the hours spent in the decision-making process, and the name of the store where the gown had been purchased. On one occasion, when the mother and daughter disagreed on a wedding detail, they sought Mrs. Adams' advice. Having worked with so many brides over the years, she always managed to resolve the issue diplomatically.

The snow continued to fall as we crept along in Mr. Adam's car, finally reaching the town of Reedville. In spite of the adverse weather, houses on both sides of Main Street exhibited the Christmas spirit. There were colored lights, homemade manger scenes, and other holiday lawn decorations.

I interrupted the silence in the car and told Mr. Adams we were about to miss the turn into Mary Jane's house. Mr. Adams, who must have also been thinking about something other than driving, just kept going. Then he realized he had missed the turn. Luckily, he was able to turn the car around without any trouble.

The porch light guided us to the side entrance of the house, where Mary Jane's mother stood in the open doorway ignoring the falling snow that covered her head and shoulders. We entered the house carrying armloads of gifts and were directed into the living room, where we found the long tables covered in white table cloths. Having made two previous deliveries, we knew the gifts were to be placed on the tables carefully next to the bridal registry and the other gifts on display.

The ride back to Kilmarnock was uneventful. The store had closed two hours earlier, yet Mrs. Adams was still working at her desk. She looked up with her glasses resting on the tip of her nose and asked how the trip had been. Before we could answer the question, she motioned us to the counter where there was a platter of her homemade *Hello Dolly* cookies and a punch bowl filled with her eggnog. We then delighted in telling her how the gifts were displayed, and that both the mother and Mary Jane had been pleased to see us again. She smiled.

Now Mary Jane, like her mother and so many others both before and after her, had become an Adams Bride. I joined their ranks later when I became and Adams Bride.

25

MISS ENID AND FAMILY

Photo 38 Enid Turner
Greenbrier Hotel, West Virginia

A black-and-white photo taken in the early 1920s shows a young woman sitting on the back steps of an old building. Her plain open-neck dress has a long tie that rests at her ankles. A closer examination of the photo reveals the young woman's hair pulled back into a stylish bun. A man stands next to her, with hands on his hips, dressed in a white dress shirt with rolled-up sleeves, a necktie, and a felt cap. On the back of the picture a pencil scribbling says "our wedding day." The bride, Enid Edmonds, was born into the old local Virginia family of Eubanks and raised in Kilmarnock. The groom was Mr. Edwin Turner, a native of Westmoreland County.

Enid Edmonds Eubank Turner, a Grand Dame of the Northern Neck

It has always been unclear to me how Miss Enid and Mr. Turner met, but until her death, she regarded herself as being his widow, even though their time together as man and wife was brief. When Laura Anna, their only child, was asked about her parents, she spoke of her mother as having been frightened by her father's seizures, an illness he suffered with all his life.

In the late 1920s, Mrs. Turner left her husband and moved back to her family home on Church Street. She and her daughter, Laura Anna, moved in with her parents, Mr. and Mrs. Willie Eubank (Silas William Eubank) and her bachelor stepbrother, Rob Sherman.

Mrs. Turner's English gardens became her prize possessions. On a typical gardening day, she could be seen wearing her garden gloves and a wide-brimmed straw hat as she toured her yard, accompanied by the schoolboy she employed. Her strolls were short, with sudden stops at the flowerbeds, where she discussed the work to be done. Gardening was a passion with Mrs. Turner, but her bad back forced her to rely on someone else to perform the hard labor.

I was a fourteen-year old girl when I first noticed Mrs. Enid Turner, her daughter Laura Anna, and son-in-law Joe, who attended the same church as my family, Grace Episcopal. Each Sunday morning this mother-daughter duo appeared in their very finest clothes and accessories--large brimmed hats with a little tilt to one side, garnished in ribbons and matching flowers. In my eyes the hats were spectacular and unforgettable.

Later I was told Mrs. Turner had once co-owned the millenary shop in her father's and uncle's store. When her father died, she and her half-brother, Rob Sherman, inherited "lots of land" and buildings in Kilmarnock, as well as farms in Lancaster and Northumberland counties. She then became the prestigious local business woman known as Miss Enid.

Any visitor who entered the back door of Miss Enid's house would find this lady sitting in her rocking chair properly dressed, wearing makeup, with her nails well-manicured.

By the 1950s this Kilmarnock icon had become a mentor and advisor to many local business owners. They sought her sound business advice on matters such as, "Do you think I should expand the inventory, add on to the building, retire, or when my lease comes due, should I buy your property?"

Each evening, she prepared supper for her family: Rob, Laura Anna, and her husband Joe. At the table, the news of the day (a nice term for "gossip") was repeated. Miss Enid told of her visitors and what news had been shared, but never would she reveal any business discussions.

She was a Sunday school teacher and active member in the church. Her strong faith was evidenced by the many handwritten prayers, poems, and thoughts she wrote.

When Grace Episcopal Church built a new church, the old members like Miss Enid made sure nothing happened to the original structure. The old church was designated as a chapel and relocated to the front of the cemetery. Miss Enid, who continued the family core values of community and generosity, donated the paint and new carpet for the little chapel. To her, privacy was an important element of generosity therefore, her name was never publicized.

Miss Enid, an avid supporter of missionary work, always put money in the mite box for Lent she kept by her bed. In the late 1930s, her church was notified a missionary was coming to Kilmarnock, and Miss Enid volunteered to host the guest. After her offer was accepted, she found out the missionary was a native of India. She then worried how to make the guest comfortable. For months before the arrival date, Miss Enid was busy researching recipes and customs of India.

When the guest arrived, she served chicken curry. Years later, when she proudly retold the story of having had a houseguest from India, her voice still reflected gratification for the experience. She would recall how the publisher of the local Warsaw paper, Mr. Morgan, contacted her to arrange for an interview with the missionary.

Not only did Miss Enid invite Mr. Morgan to her home, but she invited him to dinner. Afterwards Miss Enid received a very gentlemanly thank-you note acknowledging her warm hospitality, thanking her for having arranged the interview.

There was no mention, however, of the chicken curry, but he did include a signed 8 x 10 photograph of himself wearing a white suit and hat, addressed to both Miss Enid and Laura Anna.

Miss Enid and Mr. Rob Sherman were close siblings. They lived in the family home together (today known as The Kilmarnock Inn on Church Street).

It was after Rob's death that the family learned of his investments. He owned thirty-two row houses in downtown Baltimore that he left to his niece Laura Anna. While he did own the structures, he didn't own the land, but each property had come with a 100-year lease on it. No one knew how or why he acquired these row houses. Laura Anna decided to donate all of the properties to the Episcopal Diocese of Virginia.

**Photo 39   Rob Sherman
in his hardware tore
Main Street, Kilmarnock, Virginia**

Rob Sherman owned a hardware store on Main Street. He was a quiet and prosperous businessman. The store interior spoke of simplicity, with cans of Sherman-Williams paints on the shelves that lined the walls. A barrel in the middle of the store contained brooms and shovels that were for sale. Towards the back of the store there was a pot belly stove, a rocking chair used by Mr. Sherman, and empty nail kegs turned upside down to seat the group of local business men who visited each evening. The men smoked and exchanged the events of the day. Stories were repeated about Mr. Sherman's approach to selling.

A favorite was the story about the salesman who arrived at the hardware store and noticed all of his axe handles had been sold.

"Mr. Sherman, I see you sold all my axe handles. How many do you want to buy today?"

Mr. Sherman told the salesman he didn't want any more axe handles.

"But why, Mr. Sherman?"

Mr. Sherman responded, "Because each time someone wants to buy an axe handle, I have to leave my chair."

26

Lou Baker

Photo 40   Lou Baker

A painter's palette, never easy on the eyes, is like the characters that made my hometown rich, forgiving, humorous, and memorable. I don't recall the first time I noticed Lou Baker, but I remember him well, and how his presence made him the main character of many stories.

At the supper table one evening, Daddy shared his experience with Lou Baker earlier in the day. Daddy had picked him up hitchhiking on Route 3 to Kilmarnock. Lou didn't talk much, but smiled and nodded his head in response to Daddy's attempts at starting a conversation.

In town, after stopping the car, Daddy asked, "Lou, do you have any family?"

A smiling Lou removed the wallet from his back pants pocket and began flipping through the almost empty plastic picture holder. When he had found what he was looking for, with his right index finger he lightly tapped the center of the picture. "This is my pride and joy--my daughter," said Lou.

The picture had been cut from a magazine. Daddy immediately recognized it as a photo of Marilyn Monroe.

"She is beautiful, Lou."

The stranger, known only as Lou, became a regular in town. Everyone knew Lou as the short stocky man dressed in a black wool tattered overcoat that touched the ground. His deep, crowned black felt hat resembled those worn in the 1950s cowboy movies. As he walked and limped along aided by his wooden "staff, " his floppy brimmed hat dipped up and down, almost in rhythm with his step. People, who were accustomed to seeing Lou standing on the side of the road hitchhiking, stopped and offered him rides, which he graciously accepted. But Lou, not being a talker, never shared stories about his life. As in any small town where everyone knows everyone, Lou remained a mystery.

Lou Baker became noticeable during the early 1960s, an era when people wore only their finest clothes on Sundays. Lou's finest clothes were his only clothes---an overcoat, hat, and wooden staff. No one knew why, but Lou Baker decided to attend services at the Baptist Church in Kilmarnock. After the Sunday service, the members retreated to their education building for the social hour and were joined there by Lou. A clever Baptist took Lou aside and suggested that he visit the Episcopal Church, because they served *wine* at their communion service and offered better refreshments at their coffee hour. Lou took the suggestion to heart.

On a Sunday morning, while seated with my grandparents, I spotted Lou entering the sanctuary. As he walked up the aisle, he paused along the way, tipping his hat and nodding his head to those seated in the pews. When he reached the front row, he entered from the left side of the aisle, removed his hat, and placed it beside his staff.

Shortly after the music started, Lou reached into his coat pocket and pulled out a white handkerchief. He blew hard, not once, but several times. The displeasing sound was heard throughout the church. When he had finished, Lou shook the handkerchief and spread it over the front railing. No one noticed the altar boy leading the procession up the aisle. All eyes were on Lou.

At the end of the sermon, the "ladies" in charge of the coffee hour quietly slipped out and went into the parish house to prepare for the social that followed the service. On this particular day, my grandmother was one of those ladies who helped with the refreshments.

When Lou saw the group of ladies leave the church, he followed. Once inside the parish house, he began to eye the desserts arranged on paper lace doilies covering the silver trays.

At first no one said anything to Lou as he reached for some cookies. But then he got greedy and emptied an entire tray into his coat pockets. My grandmother saw what was happening, picked up a kitchen dishtowel, and swatted it at Lou. She went after him while Lou continued to grab more cookies and moved to the other side of the table. After she caught up to him, she announced he must leave.

Lou left, but the incident didn't deter him from adopting the Episcopal Church. Thereafter, Lou continued to sit on the front row and on communion Sundays, he was the first, after the choir, to go up to the altar and receive the communion cup. Over time people adjusted to Lou's presence. It was many years later when a church member said to my grandfather, "I truly appreciate Lou Baker, because when the minister gets too long-winded, I can always count on Lou to give a hard blow into his handkerchief. You can't get much bolder than that."

For years, Lou's house, located on Route 3 between Kilmarnock and White Stone, was in disrepair. Then it began to fall down. Someone in the community was kind enough to find a new home for Lou. He became the first white resident in the black nursing home formerly located outside of Kilmarnock. His dress and appearance never changed. For many years Lou remained a part of our local color, until one night a driver didn't see the man dressed in black, as he walked along Irvington road.

The following week Lou's picture and a short obituary appeared in our local newspaper. Of course, obituaries rarely tell the full story; therefore, Lou Baker appeared in print as just being a local who was hit by a car, and died.

27

CLAUDINE CURRY SMITH

Photo 41   Claudine Curry Smith

Miss Claudine was known locally as a courageous woman who was admired by all who knew her. In December 2005, I wrote an article about her contributions in the community when she was a midwife. I knew she was a special woman who gave so much to family, friends, church, and pregnant women. Her Grandmother had been at the bedside of my great-grandmother, Cora Lee Keane, when she died at Ditchley House. My friend, Laura Anna Turner Adams, thought the world of Claudine, who worked for both Laura Anna and her mother, Enid Turner. It was because of them and their close relationship with Claudine, I too developed an attachment.

It was a beautiful fall day when I visited Claudine. She was all dressed up and wearing her pearl necklace. She was sitting in a wheel chair when I arrived.

Claudine was eighty-two years old and still very independent. She and James Smith Sr. had been married for more than sixty years and had raised five children. She had driven a school bus for thirty-seven years, retiring in 1987.

In Claudine's presence it was hard to remember that the visit wasn't supposed to be about me. She always knew when a person was worried about something, and she made it her business to find out what it was. I was an adult in my fifties, and yet Claudine made me feel like I was only twenty. She always willingly shared her wisdom.

Claudine told me her grandmother had kept notes on herbs and had known exactly what herb to use when someone was sick. I asked Claudine if she had the notes, and I suggested we work together and get it published. I can still hear her now. "Lord, child, I don't have time to do something like that." Fearful I would ask why, she changed the subject.

"I want you to have something," she said to me. "So go over to that glass cabinet and you pick something out of it." I begged her not to make me do that, because I wanted her children and grandchildren to have her treasures.

Claudine said she was going to do what she wanted to do, and that included giving me a gift. I chose a pressed glass compote. Even today, when I think I need a "Claudine fix," I go to that compote, pick it up and then I feel better. It is almost as if Claudine is still alive.

Claudine Smith co-authored a book in 2005 with Mildred H. B. Robertson called *My Bags Were Always Packed*. In this book she describes our community when it was dependent on midwives and how, over time because of the licensing laws, the midwives slowly went away.

During our interview I asked her to tell me about how midwives looked after their patients. She said she always told her patients in advance to have hot water on the stove and a basin ready so she could wash the mother. The patients were also told to provide pads and plenty of newspapers to prepare the bed. Most of the homes, according to Claudine, were located down long dirt lanes and only had kerosene for lighting and wood stoves with which to heat.

Claudine understood the economic status of her patients. Some patients did not have the necessary supplies, so Claudine always made sure that in the trunk of her car she had clean sheets for the bed and newspapers, as well as old gowns she used to make baby clothes when waiting for the birth.

Sometimes a midwife was paid twenty dollars at the time of delivery and also given a tip. Some patients, however, volunteered to pay on the installment plan by offering five dollars a month. This was an era when "pregnancy was considered a natural occurrence not requiring medical management."

Claudine said she always devoted her attention to the patient. "I remember how I would give the patient a cup of tea, talk with her and joke as I tried to get her to relax. Once the baby arrived, if it wasn't crying after being slapped on its buttock, I'd get two pails of water, one lukewarm and one cold. I'd dip the baby first in one, then in the other four or five times. I got this advice from one of my grandmothers and a great aunt, who both had been midwives. So I thought if it was "old timey" advice, then I was gonna try it, and sure enough--it worked. And too, you kind of started by saying a silent prayer to God."

Some years later when Claudine passed away, she left her husband and children to carry on without her. I attended the viewing. Inside Calvary Baptist Church, there were many people of both races. The large screen television showed a slide show of Claudine Smith. I walked up to the casket. There lay a beautiful woman, dressed in a gorgeous silk gray suit and a matching wide-brimmed hat. Her body would leave this earth in well-deserved style. I am proud to have known this strong woman, who gave so much to our community.

28

BORN INTO THE FUNERAL BUSINESS

Photo 42   Campbell's Funeral Home

The town of Kilmarnock, population five thousand, located in the Northern Neck of Virginia is a small rural area on the Chesapeake Bay about 50 miles north of Norfolk, Virginia, 80 miles east of Richmond, Virginia, and 200 miles south of Washington, D.C. Today descendants of families who arrived here in the early 1600s still exits.. Until the discovery of the Northern Neck by recreational boaters and fishermen in the

1960s, survival depended on family-owned farms, commercial fishing, and crabbing.

Even today, there is no major industry other than menhaden fishing and no rail transportation. Everything comes into the area via vehicle and barge. It is a modern day "cocoon" for retirees who enjoy living on the water and playing golf. There are two funeral homes in town--Curry and Curry and Campbell's Funeral Home. Their history is a part of everyday living.

On Bluff Point Road, just before the stop sign that intersects Route 200, Campbell Funeral Home is located on the right side of the road. I remember my grandfather introducing me to the previous owner, Mr. Quinton Campbell. In 2003, after I retired and returned here, when driving into town, I took note of the well- dressed woman leaving the funeral home, crossing Bluff Point Road and entering a residence. After I decided to write a story about the Campbell Funeral Home, it took several attempts, but finally I managed to meet Brenda Campbell, and she agreed to share her story.

Her first words were, "I was born into an all-male family funeral home business." Brenda was a successful third-generation family business owner whose grandfather, William McKinney "Mac" Campbell established The Campbell Funeral Home in 1919. This became the first African-American funeral home in Northumberland County. In the beginning it was located in the community of Lynhams, which is now called Bluff Point; but in 1939, the funeral home moved to its present location.

Before funeral homes existed, in the early days, when a person in the black community died, Brenda's grandfather would "shroud" the deceased, a process of washing and dressing the body in preparation for burial. Brenda said the people who were well respected in the community had conducted this process with love and care. In those days, a body had been laid out in bed at home until the day of burial. Because there were no methods for preserving the body, burial occurred as quickly as family members could gather. If the deceased died in the winter, the funeral could be delayed until family and friends arrived by steamboat.

Brenda's grandfather, who also was a saw miller, made the coffins and the grave boxes. His five children, including Brenda's father Quinton, had the job of placing bedding, made from straw and unbleached muslin, in the box. Afterwards, Quinton and his sister Ruby lined the interior with pretty fabric.

Brenda spoke of how much her grandmother, Sarah Campbell, loved to raise flowers.

Always concerned there might not be any flowers at the funeral, she filled jars with water and took her flowers to the service.

In Brenda's office, on the wall hangs a picture of her grandmother Sarah Campbell. She is standing on the kitchen steps with her favorite hen at her feet.

Brenda tells the story about the night a fox got into her grandmother's hen house and ate the head off of her favorite hen. When her grandmother heard the noise, she ran into the hen house and gathered the two remaining eggs left on the nest. She carried them in her bra On Sunday morning, while everyone sat in church, a peeping sound was heard that caused Brenda's grandmother to hurriedly leave the church. Brenda said, "Those were indeed blessed chicks."

Brenda Campbell not only was born into the funeral business but raised in it as well. Her mother was a schoolteacher, so her father, Quinton Campbell, was Brenda's babysitter. Wherever he went, Brenda went with him. Everyone knew Brenda was Quinton Campbell's "daughter."

Brenda grew up knowing her father had been disappointed when told his wife had given birth to a daughter rather than a son. In later years, though, Quinton admitted he was glad to have a daughter, because if she had been a boy, he feared he may have lost her during the Viet Nam War.

When I asked Brenda how old she had been when she began to take over the Campbell Funeral Home, she responded, "about age seven." She remembers being all dressed up, wearing a hat and white gloves, standing at the head of the casket as the funeral began.

Brenda shared other memories of having grown up in the funeral home business. Once, at age nine, Brenda's father told her to ride to Richmond with a family and pick up the body of their baby from the hospital morgue. He said there would be a man at the morgue to tell her where to sign on the release papers that said, "Funeral Director or person acting as such." On that day, Brenda had been the person who acted as such, and she signed the papers.

Brenda, who graduated from Eckels College in Philadelphia, completed her studies in Mortuary Science. Following her father's footsteps, she was licensed in 1965, thus becoming the first African American woman to be a licensed Embalmer and Funeral Directress in the Northern Neck and the Middle Peninsula.

While growing up, Brenda had wanted to be a pathologist, but her father said no. She had been disappointed but says she has no regrets.

Since the first Campbell Funeral Home was established, many changes have occurred. In the earlier years, there were people in the community who had no money to pay for the services rendered to their loved ones. Therefore, they would give Brenda's father whatever they could afford--eggs, fresh vegetables, or even a cow.

Once a crying woman came to see Quinton Campbell because her sister had died, and the institution threatened to cremate the body if it wasn't picked up that day. The woman said she had no money. Mr. Campbell consoled her and said not to worry, as he would take care of everything. She was so grateful she insisted on giving him her reading glasses. Today the pair of glasses still rest on a shelf in a case at the funeral home.

Brenda said, "The glasses remind me of why I am in the funeral business. I love helping people when they can't help themselves.

On occasion Brenda has received calls from out-of-town relatives of a deceased who phoned the first name of a funeral home found in the yellow pages. When Brenda can identify the caller as being non-local, she notifies them that Campbell Funeral

Home primarily serves the black community, but is always available to everyone."

29

DITCHLEY LANDSCAPE

Photo 43   Ditchley Post Office
Ditchley, Virginia

Our small community of Ditchley included: the Goughs, a farming family of three, comprising Isabelle, a middle-aged daughter and her parents Leslie and Wheeler; two black day workers; Bobbi, my best friend; and me. All helped form the local landscape.

The Goughs

As children, Bobbi and I played hide-and-seek in Mr. Gough's cornfields. In the summer, it became hard not to pick a tomato or two from the many vines that filled Mr. Gough's fields. When I walked to Bobbi's house in the summer, I passed the black workers in the fields bent over with their legs spread apart, handpicking tomatoes in the heat of the day. A loud grinding sound from Mr. Gough's truck engine could be heard from afar.

When I first knew Mr. Gough he was old. Tall and skinny, he wore denim overalls and a brimmed straw hat. I assumed he had no teeth because he never smiled, nor did he speak. Neither Bobbi nor I liked him after he ran over Bobbi's pet cocker spaniel. The day she found her dog, the truck tire marks were still fresh on Bobbi's front lawn. A legally blind Mr. Gough didn't have a drivers' license. At least that is what the adults told us. Maybe he was blind. Maybe he was just a mean old man. I always thought the latter. I didn't really know Mrs. Gough or Isabelle, his daughter, either. These were people we just didn't see much.

Unlike the other Ditchley residents, Mr. Gough, a farmer, raised chickens, and Mrs. Gough sold eggs. She had also been our first postmistress. The post office adjoined their house. I would ride with my grandparents to the post office. Mrs. Gough greeted us with a silent nod before she handed us the mail. The frail-looking Mrs. Gough, a short, small-framed woman with gray hair pulled tightly into a bun, always wore a bib-style apron over her housedress. She never smiled. And she too seemed old.

When Mrs. Gough's health began to fail, she retired as Postmistress. Granddaddy had a one-room building that once had been his and my grandmother's first home and my parent's first home. Granddaddy moved it to the road front, where it became the last Ditchley Post Office.

Mrs. Pauline Voss, formerly my grandfather's bookkeeper, became our Postmistress. She needed a helper. When I was 13, she appointed me to be her substitute. While I worked at the post office, Isabelle Gough came in to get the family mail.

The residents, including Isabelle, customarily gathered at the Post Office around 1 p.m. to await the arrival of their mail. After the mail carrier threw the heavy, grayish, stained canvas bag up on the counter, there would still be a long wait time while the mail got sorted and each piece was placed in a designated spot. Sometimes it would be 3 p.m. before residents were handed their mail, especially during the holiday season when the mail included catalogs from Sears & Roebuck, Montgomery Ward, and Penney's.

In summer, the plump Isabelle would easily be recognizable wearing a white blouse, a homemade cotton skirt, and black sandals. She painted her toenails red. Bobby pins held her shoulder-length, reddish brown hair away from her face. I don't recall her wearing makeup other than bright orange lipstick. She smiled a lot but rarely spoke.

Once after Isabelle had picked up her mail, a newcomer who had moved to Ditchley from upper state New York said, "You know what she needs? A night out with a sailor who has just returned from nine months of sea duty." Everyone laughed and agreed that Isabelle did lead a miserable life, having to care for her parents.

At the supper table, if Granddaddy had attended a board of supervisors meeting that day, he would make a comment about Isabelle having been present at the meeting. Isabelle, a reporter, covered all county meetings and court trials for the *Northumberland Echo*. But, to the residents in Ditchley, she always would be just plain Isabelle, the daughter of old man Gough.

Mr. Gough's lane marked the halfway point between my house and Bobbi's house. At the end of the Gough's lane stood a large oak tree. This tree is where Bobbi and I met each day. After visiting with Bobbi, when it came time for us to return home we walked together to Mr. Gough's tree. And in unison, just like Dinah Shore, we sang "See the USA in a Chevrolet," threw each other a kiss, and then continued our separate ways. The tree might have been on Mr. Gough's property, but to us we owned that tree.

Whenever we met at our tree, Bobbi and I, who were faithful fans of the Mickey Mouse Club, wore our Mickey Mouse ears. Sometimes we sat under that tree and shared a movie star magazine if we had one and looked at the pictures of our favorite movie stars, Bobbi's favorite being Annette Funicello and mine Debbie Reynolds. At a younger age, each of us rode our horse, a broom. The tree is where we rested our horses after we had galloped up and down Ditchley Road in pursuit of a stray cow or a singing cowboy. It happened during these travels that we often saw Leslie or Wheeler

Leslie

Leslie, a small black man, wore a cap and rode a skinny little bike. While he rode, he chewed tobacco. Leslie worked for the caretaker at Ditchley House and looked after the chickens and the yard. Each time I would pass Leslie on

Ditchley Road, he tipped his cap and said, "Good day." I imagined he had once been a horse jockey. But the truth is-- Leslie had been a local who never left the neighborhood, and he lived with his sister, Clara, just beyond the glades.

Wheeler

Wheeler, in a child's eyes, was a giant, barefooted, black man. He wore a brimmed floppy felt hat, a shirt with rolled-up sleeves and rolled-up pants. He looked like a character that should have been on a raft poling down the Mississippi. His hat hid his face but not his white teeth, as revealed by his grin.

Most of the time, Wheeler would be "under the influence." In good weather, Bobbi and I walked all over Ditchley. Sometimes, after we had walked through freshly cut bean fields, we stopped and shared our picnic lunch on the tombstones in the old Ball cemetery. When it was asparagus season, we explored the marsh edges looking for wild asparagus to pick. If the sun was shining, each unplanned day took us outside.

Once on a hot summer day, we stumbled upon Wheeler passed out in a ditch. He lay there smelly and motionless with his mouth open, while flies swarmed about.

Our surprise reaction caused Wheeler to wake up, somewhat.

He tried to sit up, which really frightened us, because we had thought he was dead. We ran away as fast as we could.

Bobbi and I both knew Wheeler would never harm us, but from that day forward, we were more cautious during our explorations.

30

SOME MORE EQUAL THAN OTHERS

Photo 44   1960 Waiting Room sign

My reflections of how life was when I grew up here made me realize I had lived in a community of separatism.

When writing this book, I asked several people, both blacks and whites that had been born here and never lived anywhere else, if we were different from other places in the South where the Ku Klux Klan had existed. My sources were people whom I had known all of my life. One person recalled having been in a car at night with her parents when they passed a burning cross in a field near Callao. That night her parents refused to comment on what she had seen, the topic never to be discussed again.

I asked a local businessperson if he knew anything. He advised me not to bring up the subject and said, "You don't need to go there." The last person I asked said, "Yes. It is here, but that is all I am going to say." Her eyes shifted from looking directly at me to staring down at the floor.

When I mentioned these reactions to another individual, she said her husband had wanted to research this topic, but had gotten the same reaction I had received. Later I used Google on the internet, but the search resulted in nothing. So, either the presence of the Ku Klux Klan is a best-kept secret or is just a rural legend.

Looking back on race relations during the 1950s, I concluded our good life had not been flawless, because we were in reality practitioners of segregation. While I had been raised to respect all people, and had even visited in the homes of blacks, this only occurred because my daddy was unusual and saw beyond the color of a person's skin. As one black man told said, "Your daddy was color blind."

Socially, there was always an invisible line that no one from a respected white family dare cross, which meant no socializing with blacks. Still, today in our community, except for the schools, we remain segregated by choice. All-black churches, white churches, black neighborhoods, and white neighborhoods exist. A few neighborhoods do have the presence of one or two black families or a mixed racial couple living in what would otherwise be called a "white" neighborhood.

Even local white restaurants only have a few black patrons. There have been no "black" Holly Ball debutants or "black" members in the local country club. Very few blacks attend the private schools in our community. Maybe it is unfair for me to suggest separatism still exists here, because we do have a greater percentage of white residents with higher economic status than most black residents. Still, I can't help but wonder, if we had experienced more social interaction between the races, could we have all become color blind like daddy?

I only recall racial problems occurring twice in our peaceful community. The first happened in the 1960s when there were race riots in Washington, D. C. Rumors ran rampant that there would be a march and looting in Kilmarnock. When Dr. King was assassinated, a group of sympathizers marched peacefully in Kilmarnock while they mourned the loss of this great civil rights leader.

The second incident happened at a time when I was living away from here but had been coming back every other weekend. A white man shot and killed a black man who had been dating his sister.

The black community was upset and thought the white man would not be brought to trial. The white businessmen, fearful of their stores being looted, issued a call-to-arms. They spent the night with loaded shotguns protecting their stores. A rock was thrown from a car on Main Street that hit the small display window in Adams Jewelry Store in Kilmarnock.

This incident and the perceived threat of violence resulted in heavy law enforcement patrol for the next twenty-four hours. When the date of the trial was set, everything quieted down, and life returned to normal.

In 2013, I attended the ceremony sponsored by the Kilmarnock Museum for the unveiling of the state marker that recognizes the accomplishments of Dr. Morgan E. Norris. Dr. Norris believed in taking care of people. He put the needs of all people, blacks and whites, before his own.

The book, *Fight on My Soul,* written by his son, Dr. James E. C. Morgan, MD, tells of the documented efforts he made while trying to help everyone in the community. Dr. Norris, who took care of anyone who showed up at his door, could have gone to jail for treating white people. He was a brave person, because the threat of going to jail versus doing the right thing never deterred him.

Dr. Norris had been my father's doctor. When I finished reading the book, I was ready to start a campaign to have a statue erected in the town of Kilmarnock that praised his dedication to helping the community. I was pleased when I learned that the community was doing the right thing by working to recognize Dr. Norris.

Photo 45 Dr. Morgan Norris and his son and grandson at the dedication service honoring his father, Dr. Morgan Sr.

On the day of the dedication ceremony, I took a seat on the back row under the tent. The rest of the row was empty. A woman with a beautiful smile came over and asked if she could join me. After sitting there for a few minutes, I felt a connection to this woman. I thought I might have met her before.

So I asked, "Do I know you? Maybe we have been in the same writing class together."

She gave a pleasant response of "no."

We had about twenty minutes before the ceremony would begin. So we talked. She explained that she had brought her mother, who had been living with her and her husband in California, home to die. She said she had been born and raised here, but left when she started attending Hampton Institute.

After graduating from college, she had never come back except for short visits. Now she lived on the twenty-six acres her grandfather owned. Her husband, who was a white man and a three-generation Californian, was in the process of moving here, too. There was a moment when I had to ask, "Do you think he will be able to accept the separatism that exists here?"

This question started a conversation about growing up in the 1950s. She and I are the exact same age. We discovered we had lived two miles apart. Yet, because her family never worked for my family, I didn't recognize her family name. I attended white schools, and she went to black schools. When she went to high school, she attended Central High in Northumberland County, fifteen miles from her home. I went to Lancaster High School four miles from my home. She had no choice about which high school to attend. I did.

We shared our childhood memories. She recalled the time when blacks were not welcome in the local restaurant in town. She said life had definitely changed since she left here, because the other day a black waitress at Lee's Restaurant in Kilmarnock had waited on her. I told her that two months earlier that waitress had waited on me and said it was her first day on the job. We laughed and agreed change is slow around here.

I shared my frustration at not being aware of the separatism that existed when I was growing up. Back then life seemed good and normal. This lovely lady said, "They never talked about it. I grew up in Calvary Baptist Church. The topic of race was not to be discussed. That's just the way it was."

What a wonderful twenty minutes of conversation! After the ceremony, we went our separate ways. I was in pursuit of having Dr. Norris sign his book for me. It was later when I realized I did not know the name of my seatmate, yet she was a local who had lived only two miles from where I grew up and from where I live today. Our separate worlds had kept us apart. While driving home, I asked myself, "Will I ever get a chance to talk to this woman again?" She was a delightful person, yet it seemed so unreal to have found a black contemporary that had lived here when separatism was at its peak.

About the Author

Gwen Keane was born and raised in the Northern Neck of Virginia. She earned a BA in Business Administration from Trinity University, in Washington D.C. and graduated cum laude from Georgetown University, in Washington D.C. where she received her Masters' Degree in Public Administration.

Most of Gwen's thirty-four years of federal career was spent as a civilian employee with the U.S. Navy, with ten years as the Deputy Inspector General for the Naval Sea Systems Command. She received two Department of Navy Superior Civilian Service Awards, the Navy Civilian Meritorious Award and the Department of Defense Hammer Award, for her outstanding accomplishments in performance management.

Gwen, a guest speaker at two international quality performance conferences presented papers on the successes of applying the Malcolm Baldrige Award performance criteria in nonprofit organizations. She served as a Baldridge Examiner with the Department of Commerce for four years and as an examiner for the Department of Army Quality Awards Program, and the Department of Veteran Affairs Quality Awards Program.

She has been a freelance writer since 2003. Her column One of Life's Moments appears regularly in the magazine *Chesapeake Style*. She has also been published several times in the magazine *Pleasant Living*.

Gwen is the author of the non-fiction book *Swan Wait*, a personal journey with Mute Swans. She and her husband provided all of the photography that appears in the book.

Gwen remarried in 1988, and continues to enjoy world travel with her husband. She enjoys meeting people and experiencing the unexpected, which sometimes creates uncomfortable situations that make the trip memorable and triggers a yearning to return for more. At 18 she left home to attend business school. She became one of the first female managers at the Norfolk Shipyard Yard in Portsmouth Virginia. She established the Navy's first office automation program, and served two years as a director for an international technology organization. Later she moved to Alexandria for a job promotion and was selected into the Commander's Development Program with the Naval Sea Systems Command (NAVSEA). While in the program, Gwen went to sea for six days aboard the USS America and describes the experience as Five Thousand Men and me. She participated in sea trials aboard the USS Arleigh Burke and attended the christening ceremony of the USS Miami. For ten years she led inspection teams to all of the naval shipyards. She also is a graduate of the Harvard Business School Executive Management Program. While assigned as the Acting Inspector General for NAVSEA, she was in charge of two U.S. Navy Reserve Units and conducted a Change of Command Ceremony, an almost unheard of assignment for a civilian.

Now she writes in her head during early morning walks with her dogs. She values her good health and relationships with a variety of different people, including her husband, close friends and grandchildren, as well as her animals---all are the jewels in her life.

Index of Photographs

Cover - Water Color by Joseph Adams

PHOTO 1 – THE ROAD TO DITCHLEY..3
Credit: Gwen Keane

PHOTO 2 MY PATERNAL GRANDPARENTS WITH MY FATHER (IN DIAPERS)....7
Credit: Family photo

PHOTO 3 DITCHLEY HOUSE 18
Credit: Painting by Margaret Freeman (Gwen Keane)

PHOTO 4 RED FISH THAT IS THE SUBJECT OF THIS CHAPTER.....................23
Credit: Gwen Keane

PHOTO 5 MY FATHER. I AM WEARING THE RED COWBOY BOOTS, GUN AND HOLSTER HE GAVE ME FOR MY FIFTH BIRTHDAY..............................25
Credit: Family photo

PHOTO 6 ABANDONED HOUSE ON ROUTE 200 THAT IS THE SUBJECT OF A LESSON IN GENEROSITY 33
Credit: Gwen Keane

PHOTO 7 GRACE CHAPEL KILMARNOCK, VIRGINIA 39
Credit: Gwen Keane

PHOTO 8 MAMA AND ME ON EASTER SUNDAY 41
Credit: Family photo

PHOTO 9 - THE WOODEN CROSS DECORATED WITH FLOWERS AT EASTER ...42
Credit: Family photo

PHOTO 10 CHRIST CHURCH..43
Credit: Oil Painting by Hutchinson (Family owned)

Photo 11   Mama and me in 1953 45
Credit: Family photo

Photo 12   Paint of Porter's Hill   Our favorite sledding site 48
Credit: A water color painting by Joseph H. Adams (deceased)

Photo 13 Bobbi and me on the porch. Hard to believe a few
    years later we would trade our bare feet for ball gowns. . 50
Credit: Family photo

Photo 14   Photograph of White Stone Beach 51
Credit: Grayson Mattingly

Photo 15   Nellerie Johnson and me at the Ditchley Packing
    Company 54
Credit: Family photo

Photo 16   Fuggie and me He was part of the seafood business. 55
Credit: Family photo

Photo 17   Cherry Tree in the front yard of my home in Ditchley,
    Virginia 60
Credit: Gwen Keane

Photo 18   Lonnie and Minnie Curry 64
Credit: A Curry family photo

Photo 19   Wicomico Elementary School Wicomico Church,
    Virginia 67
Credit: Gwen Keane

Photo 20   Rudy lester, teresa blevins, ann thorndike, peg fuller,
    and me 1961 69
Credit: Gwen Keane

Photo 21   Bobbi and me at the May Day Variety Show Wicomico
    Elementary School 73
Credit: Family photo

PHOTO 22   SAILBOAT RACE INDIAN CREEK..74
Credit: Family photo

PHOTO 23   FISHING BOATS 80
Credit: Family photo

PHOTO 24   MENHADDEN FISH BOAT DOCKED IN REEDVILLE, VIRGINIA 81
Credit: Gwen Keane

PHOTO 25   GWEN KEANE, MISS TEXACO CROWNED BY DEAN LOUDY 95
Credit: Rappahannock Record Newspaper

PHOTO 26- THE TALENT CONTEST AT THE 1964 MISS TEENAGE CONTEST....99
Credit: Rappahannock Record Newspaper

PHOTO 27   BEING CROWNED MISS TEXACO 100
Credit: Northumberland Newspaper

PHOTO 28   OLD FAIRFAX THEATER, MAIN STREET KILMARNOCK, VIRGINIA
  102
Credit: Rappahannock Record

PHOTO 29   FERRIS WHEEL KILMARNOCK FIREMAN'S CARNIVAL............107
Credit: Gwen Keane

PHOTO 30   CONSIGNMENT SHOP CHARTES STREET, NEW ORLEANS,
   LOUISIANNA 112
Credit: Gwen Keane

PHOTO 31   THE SHOE LIKE THE ONE WORN BY MRS. WADDY 117
Credit: Gwen Keane

PHOTO 32 -EMILY KEANE ON HER 90TH BIRTHDAY PLAYING THE HARMONICA
  122
Credit: Gwen Keane

PHOTO 33 - THE TONI PERMANENT...126
Credit: Jeanne Johansen

PHOTO 34 NORA AND WILLIE GEORGE 133
Credit: Gwen Keane

PHOTO 35- MOON SHINING THROUGH THE TREES IN DITCHLEY...................139
Credit: Gwen Keane

PHOTO 36 THE TURNER HOUSE   CHURCH STREET, KILMARNOCK,
     VIRGINIA...148
Credit: Family photo

PHOTO 37   JOE ADAMS AND LAURA ANNA TURNER ADAMS.....................151
CREDIT: Family photo

PHOTO 38   ENID TURNER GREENBRIER HOTEL, WEST VIRGINIA 158
Credit: Family photo

PHOTO 39   ROB SHERMAN IN HIS HARDWARE STORE.................................162
Credit: Family photo

PHOTO 40   LOU BAKER 164
Credit. Family photo

PHOTO 41   CLAUDINE CURRY SMITH 168
Credit: *My Bags Were Always Packed* by Claudine Smith and Mildred Robertson

PHOTO 42   CAMPBELL'S FUNERAL HOME...172
Credit: Gwen Keane

PHOTO 43   DITCHLEY POST OFFICE 178
Credit: Rappahannock Record

PHOTO 44   1960 WAITING ROOM SIGN 183
Credit: Jeanne Johansen

PHOTO 45 - DR. MORGAN NORRIS AND HIS SON AND GRANDSON. 187
Credit : Gwen Keane

www.ingramcontent.com/pod-product-compliance
Lightning Source LLC
Chambersburg PA
CBHW060520100426
42743CB00009B/1388